# A CHURCH IN PERIL
## Watching Catholicism Collapse

For more information:
Ponder Point Books
410 Ponder Point Drive
Sandpoint, ID 83864

Published for Mr. Sonnichsen by
BLUE CREEK PRESS
Heron, Montana 59844
www.bluecreekpress.com

Editing, proofing and interior design provided by Blue Creek Press

## Also by Richard Sonnichsen

*High Impact Internal Evaluation: A practitioner's Guide to
Evaluating and Consulting Inside Organizations*

*Evaluation in the Federal Government: Changes, Trends, and
Opportunities* (Ed. with Christopher G. Wye)

*Can Governments Learn: Comparative Perspectives
on Evaluation and Organizational Learning*
(Ed. with Frans L. Leeuw and Ray C. Rist)

*All Fish Have Bones: A Recovering Catholic's Advice
on Living a Good Life Without Religion*

*A Leaf in a Stream: Surviving Childhood, Catholicism,
Conscription, Career and Cancer*

*To my wife Sally in thanks for
her love and support.*

# A Church in Peril

## Table of Contents

# A CHURCH IN PERIL

## Watching Catholicism Collapse

**Richard Sonnichsen**

# INTRODUCTION

**The Catholic Church** has become relevant again — for all the wrong reasons. Articles critical of the Church appear weekly in national newspapers and magazines, usually adorned with a picture of Pope Francis. A grand jury in Pennsylvania has reported the abuse of thousands of children by Catholic priests. Churches are closing, priests are leaving the Church to get married, pedophile priests are being identified and prosecuted in the criminal justice system and multi-million dollar payments to victims of sexual abuse are bankrupting dioceses.

These are distressing and bewildering times for Catholicism. By any metric, the Roman Catholic Church is a church in peril, collapsing as we watch. One pope has retired, Francis has been asked to resign by one of his subordinates, and the faithful in the pews are either simply ignoring rigid Church rules governing their sex lives or leaving the pews altogether and living meaningful, secular lives. Millennials, uninterested in divine mysteries and ancient dogma, don't attend church at all and are comfortable with a temporal lifestyle. There is a frightening instability in the Catholic Church today.

# A CHURCH IN PERIL

The Church faces a colossal and complicated challenge. Churches and schools are being shuttered and priests are leaving the Church; ominous symptoms of significant problems. The Church is confronted with corrupt clergy members committing criminal, abusive acts against helpless children, a disgusted laity and a thriving, youthful generation that has little use for divine guidance, organized religion or church authority in their lives.

The Catholic Church is facing the greatest moral challenge in its history. Clinging steadfastly to ancient, outmoded dogma, the Church seems unable to seriously confront the malignant child abuse scandal among its clergy. It is also reluctant to address a flawed recruitment process for candidates for the priesthood and challenged by a corrupt, feckless and divided leadership among bishops and Vatican prelates.

The Church seems morally adrift — out of touch with the modern world and evasive with the constituency it supposedly serves. It is apparently impotent, mystified and without a resolution to a complicated and thorny state of affairs. The Catholic Church is undergoing a serious legitimization crisis, eroding internally and externally. It is collapsing and becoming unmoored from its core mission: teaching love, compassion and salvation.

It's difficult to reconcile the Catholic message of God's love and compassion for all His creations while priests are molesting innocent children. The cover-up of the pederasty scandal in the Church only intensifies the serious nature of the situation. The Catholic Church is facing significant management and ethical issues and is perilously close to losing its moral authority and ability to faithfully serve its constituents.

The Church's continued allegiance to a medieval mentality and world view and its ancient dogma makes it difficult to address the pedophile issue with a creative, intellectual attitude and modern management tools. And, the challenge for the Church is more than just a solution to the pedophile issue. It needs to examine its doctrines and practices to determine if they are relevant in modern times.

According to O'Dea, "The sociological demythologization of the Church involves the dismantling of this vast superstructure, the disentangling of its essential, timeless elements from their historically and culturally conditioned expressions, and their new institutionalization. It is a process fraught with conflict, danger, and suffering, but it is the price of vitality and relevance."

If the Church is to survive and remain relevant it must make significant and bold changes to its recruitment practices, doctrinal issues and institutional and authority structure. The Church, with its historical hegemony collapsing, has slowly been rendered peripheral in an enlightened, modern world. Any reformative paradigm shift, however, comes at the expense of undermining and possibly nullifying the core doctrines of the Church!

We are the big-brained species but we don't always use our brainpower productively. The human mind has evolved to try to make sense of the world — to acquire a sense of purpose and meaning. But we seem unable to use it constructively and analytically when it comes to pondering the mysteries of the supernatural. Our ancestral nature was incubated in superstition and ignorance and it needs to be reexamined in light of contemporary knowledge. The current turmoil and confusion plaguing the Church presents an appropriate opportunity for Catholics to examine their affiliation with Catholicism and belief in Church doctrine and policies. It is intellectual stubbornness to refuse to entertain a rational inquiry into religious doctrines that guide your life.

Criticizing religion, although gaining some traction, is still not a popular pursuit, but the world runs on ideas. You are what you think and what you think is important. Equally important is how you feel about yourself. Are your philosophical beliefs really uniquely yours and are you comfortable with them?

Questioning sacred religious concepts that many believe have a Divine origin and applying a secular viewpoint to explain reality is not always considered intellectual enlightenment. It is often judged as insulting to Christians and critics are assigned to hellfire. Disparaging religious beliefs is often considered offensive, and rational discourse is beyond the capacity of many pious believers, but failure to challenge the precepts of the origins of Christianity is intellectual lethargy.

No idea, concept or orthodoxy should ever become so enshrined in people's minds that it cannot be challenged. Ideas, traditions, axioms, myths, concepts and theories are not immutable, monolithic convictions that should never be questioned. Rather, they should be periodically subjected to examination and enlightened scrutiny to determine their current verity and usefulness to society. Unfortunately, by claiming mystical, transcendental, supernatural properties not of this world, religion has conveniently excluded itself from rigorous evaluation and seemingly has become immunized to scrutiny.

I believe it's imperative for those holding alternative views of religion to encourage thoughtful analysis of the issues, challenge conventional norms and promote debate among diverse viewpoints. In the universe of human experience, some ideas are able to be proven and others are products of the imagination. Questioning the superstitions and primitive beliefs of early Christians is intellectually challenging but enlightening when it exposes fundamental flaws in venerable precepts of faith.

Developing intellectual habits that challenge dubious religious claims is a step toward emancipation. My motive for writing this book is to stimulate individuals to reclaim or establish thought processes that may have been suffocated for most of their lives by faith in spurious religious dogma. Deep reflection and introspection may reveal a religious practice that is no longer suitable. I would like to introduce readers to a viable alternative to traditional Western Christian culture that may be more relevant as guidance for a productive and happy life than long-established, conventional religious beliefs.

I was born religious. The zygote that eventually became me received 23 Lutheran chromosomes from my father and 23 Catholic chromosomes from my mother, a DNA profile replicating the Protestant Reformation! For all practical purposes, though, I was raised, educated and immersed in Catholicism, the religion of my mother. Achieving escape velocity from those childhood religious beliefs took seven long decades of nominal attention to Church doctrine and rote attendance at Sunday mass — until I finally became aware of the numerous flaws in religious belief.

It never occurred to me that someday I would not be Catholic. I accept the fact that it was my responsibility to take charge of my own life philosophy, but I resent the inordinate amount of time it took me to apply reason and common sense to Catholic doctrine, tradition and practice. My feeble excuse is that my education, military service, career, wife and family occupied all my time, and I never allocated any space for a contemplative review of the doctrines of the Church until I retired. Hopefully, my writing and observations will assist others to arrive at conclusions similar to mine earlier in their lives. I spent far too much unproductive time in church. Hopefully I can spare others that same fate.

For better or worse, we are forever shaped by our childhood experiences. My lengthy association with the Church is best characterized as the result of a distorted childhood legacy, a gloomy apprenticeship in the Catholic faith. Because of my childhood environment, I bonded with Catholicism, which implanted an invisible influence in me that was difficult to erase. The legacy of one's youthful environment is almost intractable and will linger long into adulthood. Reflecting on my past, I believe I spent more time during my childhood in the presence and influence of nuns and priests in school and church than I did with my parents.

You cannot exit your mind but you can periodically examine its contents to determine if they are compatible with reality. It is challenging for people to transform their views from believing in a promise of eternal salvation to the pragmatics of natural existence with a permanent ending. One of the sublime satisfactions in life is to confront the guilt complex, myths and demons from childhood religious experiences and excise them from the perspective and contentment of maturity and an enlightened intellect.

I was a Catholic for a very long time. A conservative estimate of my attendance at Sunday Masses would be 3,500. Some of the feedback I received from readers of my book, *All Fish Have Bones: A Recovering Catholic's Advice on Living a Good Life Without Religion*, was that I appeared to be angry at the Catholic Church. That is a correct assessment. There is an exasperating nature to religion that is not always immediately apparent. I was angry at the Church for its message of guilt, rigid doctrines and irrational view of the world. The Catholic tradition of my youth had a baked-in pessimism. I'm still irritated, but I shoulder much of the blame since I could have arrived at a decision to leave the Church much earlier in my life if I had devoted the time and energy to study and evaluate Church doctrine and promises.

I attended Mass on Sundays out of habit for seven decades, even searching out churches while on vacation. I was educated exclusively by nuns for 12 years, baptized, confirmed and married in the Church. My wife has 16 years of Catholic education. I am a Third Degree Knight of Columbus. My wife and I donated money and time to church requests, listened to boring homilies characterizing us as sinners and confusing us with the rigid sexual policies promulgated by the Church. Church rituals — Sunday Mass, communion, confession, fasting, abstaining from meat products on Fridays — were part of everyday life. Fear of God's wrath and everlasting punishment for committing sins and the corresponding guilt were conspicuous components of Catholic life. Recommended weekly confession was employed by the Church as a reminder of the shame and guilt that were prominent themes of Catholicism.

Leaving the Church can be precipitous or measured. Some leave abruptly because of remarks by a priest or a personal policy dispute that can't be resolved. Others grow disenchanted over a longer period of time. For me, leaving the Church was not tied to any identifiable event, nor was it based on the personality of any single priest. My interest in leaving the Church began with a gradual recognition that the doctrines were illogical and lacked any supporting evidence. I concluded that the life I had was the only life I was ever going to have and the potential for a second blissful existence somewhere in the cosmos was highly improbable. I wish this epiphany had occurred sooner.

I have lived for quite a long time; not as long as the Old Testament figures whose ages ran to hundreds of years, but a substantial span for modern man. As a newly minted octogenarian, I am very much aware of the time I may have left. The horizon of my mortality is coming into view — fuzzy but still discernable. Many of my friends, golfing partners and work associates have passed away and daily obituaries are reminders of the obvious. According to actuarial tables, a male born in 1939 (my birth year) has a life expectancy of 62.1 years. By that standard, I am quite successful. Hopefully that trend continues. Birthdays are cause for celebration.

# Introduction

One of my primary motives for writing this book is to alert readers to the potential for reviewing their connection to organized religion and determine if it satisfies their current needs. Most of us have periodical physical check-ups to examine the status of our health. We should also periodically assess our mental wellbeing. I would hazard a guess that many of us skip this examination and continue on the rote path of our childhood beliefs. We are connected to organized religion only because we always were and never thought much about it. Hopefully, this book will prompt readers to thoughtfully and objectively examine their religious beliefs and decide if they are rational and still make sense in the modern era. Applying sound reasoning (Cartesian logic) to religious doctrines will expose their flaws and contradict some of what you have been told by religious authorities.

I have no wish to criticize strongly held personal religious beliefs or anyone's version of a God or afterlife. My goal is to stimulate questioning in those who may harbor doubts about their religion or who are interested in an intellectual examination of the role of religion in their lives and in society. Hopefully, this book will motivate inquiring minds to search religious literature, read alternative explanations of life on Earth and facilitate an introspection of ingrained religious doctrines. English novelist E. M. Forster (1879-1970) wrote in *Two Cheers for Democracy* (1951), "The only books that influence us are those for which we are ready and which have gone a little farther down our particular path that we have yet gone ourselves." My hope is that my books will nudge readers to go a little farther down the path of religious belief and see if they can discover some provocative and stimulating ideas that may change their attitude toward familiar and traditional religious doctrines.

Religion is irrational faith in an unrealistic abstraction with no observable supporting evidence and impossible odds that it is true. What is remarkable is that never in human history have so many people believed in an impractical idea with virtually no detectible or verifiable indicators that it is anything more than a persistent myth.

In this book, I will look more in-depth at the origin of the Catholic religion, its fragile founding premise and the reason for its persistence. My interest in studying this religious phenomenon is sustained by indignation at myself for failure to recognize earlier the flaws in religious doctrines and the reasons for the persistence of religious belief. I am trying to discover why religion has not disappeared. Instead, it continues to prosper in the face of substantial scientific evidence explaining Biblical assertions without the use of supernatural intervention.

One problem in writing about religion is that there are no definitive answers to its impossibly ambiguous answers to existential questions and inadequate language to accurately convey the meaning of supernatural events. Since humans have no linkage with the supernatural, religious events and doctrines are subject to individual interpretation and expressions in human language. The end result is portrayal of a mystical deity in anthropomorphic language.

Since the beginning of recorded history, humankind has gravitated toward tribal living, attracted by the benefits of living with a like-minded group and the comfort of a static and predictable existence. Religion fits this phenomenon with its preference for stability over change — a condition that could also be described as chronic stagnation. Embracing ancient religious beliefs gave ancients hope, solace and an explanation for natural events occurring in the world. What we now consider flawed and outmoded doctrine was, for a primitive audience, sufficiently plausible and rational. Religion has outlived its usefulness as an explanatory trope for interpreting natural events to primitive minds.

Like an ancient bug entombed in amber, the Catholic Church is stuck in its archaic dogma. Its ability to endure has been facilitated by written verse in the Bible, historical traditions and the tantalizing but unfulfilled promise of another life. In this book I hope to establish that Catholicism has been a flawed philosophical belief from the beginning and the current turmoil exposes the defects in both doctrine and ministry. The dogmas the Church has preserved since antiquity deserve to be evaluated for both their verity and their relevance in modern times.

I believe we are entering a watershed time in Catholic history when the Church will be challenged to examine and determine the relevance and necessity of its doctrines against modern developments in science, philosophy, values, morality and ideals. The moral authority of the Church is at stake and the available evidence points to a church perilously close to collapse.

With the exclusion of some religious cults, evil is not traditionally attributed to a religious organization. However, the malevolence and immorality we are observing in the Catholic Church makes "evil" a suitable adjective to describe current circumstances of the Church. When I was growing up in the Catholic faith, it was unthinkable that a priest could harm and destroy a young life. But it happened. We are watching the gradual collapse of Catholicism. ◆

# A CHURCH IN PERIL

# CHAPTER ONE
# A Mystifying Origin

**Roman Catholicism, one** of the oldest faith traditions, had a mystifying origin. Its founder was purportedly a carpenter from Nazareth named Jesus who preached a message of brotherly love and salvation for only three years before he was accused of insurrection by Roman authorities and crucified. His immediate followers were illiterate and failed to leave any written record of their experiences. Jesus himself wrote nothing — zero.

We know very little about Jesus' youth, education or travels. Yet, in the taxonomy of men who have influenced history, Jesus of Nazareth stands distinctively apart from all the others. His preaching was the origin of Christianity.

Some think his life was only a myth, but whether he lived or not is not as important as his impact on the world. The significant issue here is not whether or not Jesus was a real person, but the impact of his existence — alleged or not — on subsequent generations.

## A CHURCH IN PERIL

The entire history of the planet was once separated into two periods, before Christ was born (BC) and after Christ was born (AD, for Anno Domini). We now use BCE (before common era) and CE (common era), but the dividing point is still the reckoned time of the birth of Jesus.

I believe his message was more important than the man. The global influence of Jesus' message is unmatched in human history. He presents a smorgasbord of images, the meaning of which depends on the perception of the viewer. He was a self-proclaimed messiah who allegedly cured the sick and raised the dead. But for the major influence he has had in the universe, almost nothing is known about him. His is an indistinct presence that is difficult to visualize, understand or imagine.

According to the story, the carpenter from Nazareth was born in Palestine in an undistinguished, unassuming and unpopulated desert setting. His message gained traction with the primitive people of the time — and continues to attract followers 2,000 years into the current era. He was viewed as having a double identity — both human and divine, mortal and immortal. He preached a message of love and forgiveness and claimed to be the son of the one true God. He spoke of a God who was never born and would never die, but gave few further details that would help us understand this God. He promised a second coming when He, as God, would come down to Earth in glory and splendor and save the righteous and condemn the sinners. Two thousand years have passed since that utterance, and the odds are long that it will ever happen.

English philosopher Thomas Hobbes (1588-1679) described human life in the 16th century as solitary, poor, nasty, brutish and short. This description can also be applied to life in the first century. They too led marginal, disenfranchised lives. Jesus' message of a better life ahead resonated with a poor, uneducated, superstitious people living insignificant existences. In a life filled with uncertainty, misery, anxiety and ignorance, the powerful imagery of Jesus' message was a welcome alternative to the drudgery of daily existence. The longings and hopes of those people would have been buoyed by the concept of a better life awaiting them in the beyond — the theology of expectation.

2

Jesus' astonishing claim that he was the son of God sent to save the world has reverberated throughout history with countless positive and negative consequences. Jesus portrayed a miraculous world unlike the one his audience was enduring. It may have been a dubious promise, but it offered eventual escape to a better world, a belief that present lives would improve at the end. Even though Jesus offered no evidence whatsoever for his claims, uneducated people living at that time were easily seduced by a charismatic prophet who promised a superior life in the future — a life after life.

Real life presents us with a wealth of unknowns and an abundance of things to fear. Fear and uncertainty lead many to embrace religion to assuage emotions, diminish anxiety and make some moral sense of the world they live in. Religion can act as a psychological lubricant. Sharing a collective experience like religion with others validates our existence and gives us a sense of belonging to something greater than ourselves. However, religion can be a net negative in our lives. We need to ask some nettlesome questions about the value of religion.

Who is God? Did He create the world? Does He matter in our lives? Does religion make us better or worse human beings; does it add value to our lives? Why would God create human minds that are incapable of understanding Him? Do God's creations really have a reasonable expectation of salvation — a heavenly afterlife? Has Christian ideology been beneficial in the progress of humankind? Does conformance to the rigid rules and regulations of Christianity help humans cope with their lives? Is religion an essential component of our culture worth preserving? Do we need a sense of the Divine to exist? Is God a useful concept?

The broad theological framework of Christianity is that God was revealed to humans in Jesus of Nazareth. Christianity introduced the idea of Jesus as man and divine being and the concept of a triune God — Father, Son and Holy Ghost. However, the formative history of the Catholic religion has a porous foundation based on superstition, fable and a primitive knowledge of the universe. It is wholly dependent on unknowable, supernatural phenomena for explanation.

If one is committed to a particular philosophy of life, it should be supported by robust principles, prominent moral values and convincing scientific evidence that conforms to the existing laws of nature and undergirds solid epistemological assumptions. Religion does not meet any of these criteria. Religion and reality collide at the intersection of myth and reason. Seeking the rational view involves searching for a truth supported by evidence, experience and observation.

Religion is the sublime art of stating a myth authoritatively and repeatedly until it slowly acquires the status of fact. It creates an intricate web of myths loosely hung together (by human craving for immortality). It blurs the boundaries between fantasy and reality. Faith is something that cannot be rationally established, so religion dazzles the imagination with images and concepts of ineffability and mystery.

Christianity can easily be described as a "cult." Cults are described by sociologists as movements that have a charismatic leader, a convincing message — true or not — and fulfill the needs of the followers. Reality, on the other hand, can be determined as truth with a dogmatic assertion of certainty.

Shermer defines religion as:"…a social institution that evolved as an integral mechanism of human culture to create and promote myths, to encourage altruism and reciprocal altruism, and to reveal the level of commitment to cooperate and reciprocate among members of the community." Religion is a gateway drug to a long-term dependency on a delusional belief in the supernatural.

Jesus and his followers were bound together by their primitive culture and his promise of a future improved life. Jesus intimated that he and his Father lived in an alternate universe where everything was perfect. He promised his listeners they could go there after death if they believed in him, payed him homage, obeyed his commandments and were respectful of each other.

Jesus' message was substantial in concept but crumbly, suspicious and sketchy in detail. He did not say where this extraordinary place was, what it was like or how you traveled there — just that you had to die before you could begin the journey. He never described God, although God allegedly was his father.

"God…is this kind of a living question mark — a wholly prospective character. He has no history, no genealogy, no past that in the usual way of literature might be progressively introduced into his story to explain his behavior and induce some kind of catharsis in the reader." (Miles)

Let's objectively examine the origin and core elements of the Catholic religion. Jesus of Nazareth was, according to the story, an illiterate carpenter turned prophet. Almost nothing is known about his early life. At about age 30, he began preaching peace and good will among people on Earth. He believed he was sent by God, whom he proclaimed was his father. He said for those who believed his message there would be a celestial reward after death and a corresponding punishment for those who failed to adhere to God's commandments. After three years of preaching, Jesus was crucified by the Roman authorities for insurrection — at the behest of the Jewish hegemony, whose power he challenged.

The emotional and inescapable implication of Jesus' redemptive death — "there is no redemption except by blood" — and subsequent alleged resurrection were the beginnings of Christianity. The ghoulish scene depicting Jesus' crucifixion has been rendered a powerful, emblematic abstraction over time by the conspicuous usage of the cross as an iconic symbol of Christianity.

History does not reveal any information about Jesus' life between his birth in Bethlehem and the beginning of his public ministry at the age of 30. What was he doing and where was he for 30 years? I am surprised that his physical appearance has never been described. Why don't we know how tall he was, his weight, color of hair and features? Those facts should have survived the oral transmission to the Gospels. Why would a loving God — originator of the universe — create followers who couldn't understand Him and have His son speak in obtuse parables to an uneducated audience? Jesus' message revealed a certain degree of intelligence. Where did he receive his education? Who influenced him? Why did his supernatural father allow him to be crucified for sins that were never committed?

Jesus and his followers were illiterate and left no written examples of their thinking, judgements or beliefs. Anyone could interpret the oral tradition that survived and fashion it to suit their own agenda. The confusing message of salvation and punishment was hijacked by the Patristic writers, particularly Paul and Augustine. These two misanthropic misogynists substituted asceticism, sexual repression, the inferiority of women and the concept of Original Sin as central doctrines of Christianity. Unfortunately, this flawed view of life on Earth escaped thoughtful review by Church authorities for centuries and remains the nucleus of Catholic Church teaching in spite of copious evidence to the contrary.

Judaism, which spawned Christianity, was the beginning of monotheism — conversion of a portfolio of gods to a single sovereign God incorporating all the attributes of the previously worshipped deities. We no longer needed a god for each naturally occurring event in the universe.

In Genesis, we learned that Yahweh is that God — the creator of the Earth and all organisms on it. Judaism, and Christianity after it, teach that humans are unique in nature and superior to all other life forms. Scripture distinguished humans from the rest of living organisms. Over time we have developed a preference for that Biblical version of ourselves.

Also, we evidently still feel a need for a divine overseer in order to live moral lives, even though morality has evolved throughout history as a cooperative mechanism to enable humans to interact with each other in a productive way. The evidence for human morality, without a divine dimension, is supported by the cooperative life within social groups. "Human morality is clearly an extension of evolved mammalian cooperation strategies and the sentiments needed to implement those strategies — sympathy, gratitude, trust, a sense of fairness, etc." (Farris Naff and Norman)

Many attitudes formed in childhood about people and the universe come from fairy tales we read or hear which contain truths, falsehoods, fears and moral principles that inspired imaginations and crystalized thinking that last into adulthood. These stories are usually set in an unfamiliar cultural environment with an underlying moral message in the narrative that is often too subtle for naïve young minds to comprehend.

Children are gullible, easily led by authority figures and particularly susceptible to believe in magical events and ideas. Their minds are like sponges, soaking up whatever they hear, read and experience. However, unlike living aquatic sponges that filter out what they don't need, children have no reality filter to separate fact from fantasy or reality from myth. Christianity is one of those fairy tales set in a foreign culture, centuries removed from modern times.

In Genesis, we learn that God created the heavens and Earth and humans to populate the Earth. Though humans and most other air-breathing organisms need to reside on land, the Earth's surface is 70 percent salt water. The ratio of land to water seems significantly out of balance for land-based creatures and could easily be cited as a creation design flaw.

Genesis, the foundation for much of Catholic doctrine, is nothing more than a whimsical fairy tale. Yet, from the story of Adam and Eve in the Garden of Eden, we derived an intriguing tale of the creation of the Earth and humankind, and then the concepts of Original Sin and shame, the image of a vengeful and deceitful God, plus gender inequality and misogyny.

The severity of punishment — banishment from paradise, daily toil and painful childbirth — was highly inappropriate and substantially out of proportion to Eve's disobedience and Adam's complicity. To condemn all of humankind forever for Eve's transgression is irrational.

Eve was chosen by biased male authors of Genesis to become the first sinner and to infect human posterity with the stain of Original Sin and eventual death. Why not choose Adam?

Blaming Eve was the first Biblical example of oppression of women by men and the origin of Judeo-Christian patriarchy. All of this was fabricated from the imagination of male writers who told the story of a fictional couple who never existed. "Evolution proves that the biblical Adam and Eve did not exist. Their 'original sin' was therefore impossible, so there would be no need for a messiah to save us from our sins." (Gray)

God's communication with His creations can only be categorized as bizarre. For the first hundreds of thousands of years of human existence the Judaic-Christian God was silent. Then, for about 1,200 years, during the period of the Old Testament, He was apparently both loquacious and personally involved with His creations. He communicated originally with Adam and Eve and then regularly with Moses, Abraham, Isaac, David, Jeremiah, Elijah and other prophets. Throughout the Old Testament we hear the disembodied voice of a God speaking to His people, giving instructions on how to live, keep His commandments and obtain salvation.

In the New Testament, He used His son Jesus as spokesperson. However, since the death of Jesus almost 2,000 years ago, His advice and admonitions have stopped and the protracted silence is deafening. Did God die? That explanation seems unlikely since He is claimed to be eternal. Did He lose interest in His creations? That seems implausible, too. You would think a creator would have at least some interest in His creations and periodically check up on how things were going.

That leaves a more plausible and logical explanation — that the God of the Bible only existed in the minds of the Biblical writers and a real God never existed.

When humans first appeared on Earth, they embarked on an intellectual and spiritual journey to understand the universe and their place in it. This quest is essentially a supernatural question; a potent and compelling undertaking.

Religion is an unnecessary intrusion into the process of living. It introduces uncertainty, adds complexity and raises more questions than it answers. Religion is counterfactual to reality. It introduces mystery, fantasy and transcendent concepts that are beyond our ken. The difficulty in defining and discussing religion is that the topic itself is subjective, mystical and unverifiable. Love, happiness and compassion are emotions that can be discussed, observed and measured in humans, but when these are attributed to supernatural spirits, the conversation departs from reality to an unseen and unknowable cosmic mystery.

We tend to attribute the founding of Christianity to Jesus, but in reality, Christianity is the result of many individuals writing and embellishing the activities and pronouncements about Jesus and his followers, early Jewish customs and myths and fantasies about primitive cultures.

For many, religion is a convenient trope to deflect mysterious happenings in the world. Religion functions for some as a security blanket, alleviating the necessity to study, analyze and think about how the world really works. "It is God's will," is a trite but handy aphorism to assign God responsibility for all the phenomena that baffle humankind. ❧

# A CHURCH IN PERIL

# CHAPTER TWO
# A Confusing Concept

**The origins of** Catholicism are shrouded in mystery. All that is required is blind faith in an unseen and unknowable cosmic entity. Historically, cultures have fashioned metaphysical belief systems to try and make sense of the world and answer the fundamental question of humanity. "In culture after culture, people believe that the soul lives on after death, that rituals can change the physical world and divine the truth, and that illness and misfortune are caused and alleviated by spirits, ghosts, saints, fairies, angels, demons, cherubim, djinns, devils and gods." (Pinker)

The phenomenon of religion is opaque and challenging to define. Religion is an illusory, emotional, theological state that requires a creative imagination, the suspension of common sense, natural laws and all the principles of science and philosophy. It is dogmatic, belief-centric and ideological. Religion is wish fulfillment, a wacky theology, a pseudoscientific belief in things we cannot see with seductive prophecies of a better future.

# A CHURCH IN PERIL

The bizarre phenomenon of Christianity is that we pay homage to an image of an androgynous God we know nothing about. This God was introduced to us as his father by a prophet we know almost nothing about. Yet we have become convinced that this notion of the supernatural is somehow factual; a confusing perception that has been accepted as truth. Religion confronts its followers with the dilemma of a contradictory relationship between the orbit of imagination and the domain of experience. Faith is the required linkage of the supernatural with the real world. To paraphrase Churchill, never in history have so many believed so much about so little.

Christianity is essentially an unsubstantiated promise of an afterlife made by an illiterate peasant in the Palestinian desert 20 centuries ago. The concept of the Christian God, developed by humans, is a deceptively simple premise: God, a supernatural being that always existed, created the universe and everything in it including humans. Humans, His special creations, will be rewarded with a second life on an astral plane somewhere if they worship Him, obey His commandments and behave in accordance with His principles. All others will be punished.

The attraction of theism often hinges on the circumstances of disenfranchised populations. The appeal to supernatural entities is usually an effort to alleviate the chronic anxiety that accompanies living a marginal existence in a chaotic world. People who are content do not feel the same attraction to religious beliefs because they are comfortable with the way they are living their lives without any help from a divine source.

Kurtz suggests in a 2002 article in *Skeptical Inquirer* that theistic beliefs may be more dependent on adult life circumstances than childhood indoctrination.

"It follows that religion is not nearly the inevitable result of how the brain works that has to be intellectually beaten out of childish gullible adults to convince them via hard science-based thought to become nonreligious. Theism is an optional opinion that often but not always is adopted by mass majorities when their life circumstances are sufficiently dysfunctional and when enough people in leadership positions are exploiting such positions to establish religious power structures. It follows then, that the discretionary opinion that is theism is easily, inevitably, and usually casually off when the life circumstances of the majority are sufficiently pleasant enough for most to no longer feel the need to go to the considerable trouble to petition powers of dubious reality."

Religion has a confusing dual narrative of life and death that minimizes secular reality and champions a remote, supernatural dimension that occurs in an unknown somewhere. Religion asserts that we are influenced by an invisible force that we can't observe and don't understand. Religion teaches us that death is not an end but a beginning — an apocalyptic scenario lurking on the horizon of life. This eschatological mindset is disorienting and distracting to gravity bound Earthlings grappling with meaning and belief in an observable and tangible environment. Religion is an exhausting, thorough emotional workout. It assures followers there is a better life ahead, but fails to deliver the emotional tools to cope with the dying, death and resurrection procedure.

The beginning of a new Catholic life may be a joyous occasion on the surface but viewed through the lens of Catholic doctrine it takes on a different perspective. According to Augustine the very act of conception is a sinful act. Add to that Original Sin and the inclination toward sinfulness that everyone inherited from Eve via her transgression in the Garden of Eden, and one has the beginning of a flawed, confusing and unrequested existence.

"In the first centuries of Christianity, asceticism was considered an appropriate practice to become closer to God. These Christians endeavored to live not for this world, but for the next. Their goals were spiritual growth and moral improvement, cultivated by prayer, charitable acts, and immersion in the Scriptures through study and discussion. Unfortunately, the thinking of Augustine has been incorporated in much of Catholic doctrine. His focus on the hereafter is especially troubling. He viewed life on earth as temporary, not a true home. He preferred to be united with his God. In his autobiography, *Confessions*, he wrote that 'we are restless hearts' longing to escape to a better place. Some Greek, Roman, and Hebrew men have extolled asceticism and followed the path themselves, but Christian asceticism went further; it extolled not only sexual continence, but sexual virginity." (Anderson and Zinsser)

"The spiritual life was based not only on the inhibition and control of the passions and drives but also upon the focusing of the mind upon otherworldly realities." (O'Dea)

The Church's historical obsession with sex is astonishing to me. The Catholic Church has always been uncomfortable with the topic of sex and has been perpetually awkward and confused when dealing with the natural sexual impulses of human nature. The Church has never appreciated the idea that humans are sexual beings and that sex is the engine of nature that maintains continuation of a species.

Sexual activities and sexual relations have always been considered evil in the eyes of the Church and sexuality has been regularly denigrated, while celibacy and chastity have been held in high esteem as the ideal approach to a spiritual life. This discomfort has manifested itself in rigid rules for sexual behavior. It is mystifying that sex is a blatantly conspicuous topic in Roman Catholic Church teachings, not because of its vital role in human affairs, but because its suppression is a core axiom of the Church.

During the fourth and fifth centuries, the Catholic Church slowly became confused about its identity and alignment with the original message of the founding prophet, Jesus. The sad, historical irony of Christianity is the stunning change from the message of Jesus to the message of Paul and Augustine. Along with other Patristic writers, they grafted nascent Christianity on to the established tree of Greek misogyny. Jesus' preachings were replaced by the ideas of Paul and the Patristic writers who appropriated Greek sexist philosophies and combined them with their own mystifying views of controlling sexual energy to form the repressive sexual teachings of the Church which are still in vogue today.

"Christianity had a profound encounter with Greek thought and came out of the experience incorporating into itself important insights of antique intellectual culture. As the Church's teachings hardened into formal doctrine and as its truly religious aspects became part of an overall philosophical view of the world, any radically new hypothesis about the fundamental nature of things was increasingly likely to be experienced as a threat to the already formulated view of man and his world." (O'Day)

Scripture is almost devoid of any discussions of sex by Jesus, yet Paul and Augustine, two ascetic men, became fixated with sexual behavior, which had profound implications on the future of Christianity. Sex was portrayed as an evil impulse to be repressed if at all possible so one could concentrate on the goodness of God. They essentially reframed the message of Jesus and replaced it with virginity, chastity and sex avoidance as central doctrines of the Church.

"Following Scripture's positive attitude to procreation, the Catholic Church teaches that a Christian should not have any sexual experience, mental or physical, outside marriage, and that within marriage procreation is never to be excluded by a deliberate act. This is a hard saying for the human race, but the doctrine is clear, logical, and consistent with Scripture." (Podles)

Catholic Church tradition generally prohibits any non-reproductive sexual activities by either homosexual or heterosexual persons. Sexual activity that circumvents the goal of procreation is prohibited. The Church has painstakingly managed to preserve this dark view of sex and has wrestled unsuccessfully with finding a balance between natural sexual expression and spirituality. The Church advocates sexual restraint and opposes premarital sex, homosexual sex, abortion, masturbation and sex for pleasure. In the eyes of the Church, responsible sex only occurs in marriage when it plays a reproductive role and non-procreative sex is sinful.

An intriguing and provocative question that Catholics should ask themselves is, "Why is the Catholic Church fixated on human sexuality and why does it feel the necessity to intrude into people's lives and try to control their sexual behavior?"

# A CHURCH IN PERIL

Retired Foreign Service officer Kohanski, writing in an intriguing article in *Humanist* magazine — "Why the Catholic Church is So Conflicted about Sex" — traces this obsession back to the Essenes. They were a Jewish sect active from the second century BCE to the first century CE. They preferred celibacy to marriage and believed sex was strictly for procreation and not for pleasure. He points out that ". . . early Christians were expecting the return of Jesus and the establishment of the kingdom of God at any moment. . . Why bother continuing to populate the world when there would be shortly no need for new human beings? And why bother to get married when there would be no sex in heaven?"

The Catholic Church is experiencing a postmodern sexual revolution. The distorted Catholic teachings on the purposes of sexuality is incomprehensible to modern minds. Living in the modern liberal era, with the advocacy of sexual liberation a common feature of many cultures, it's difficult to comprehend a continuation of the traditions of celibacy, virginity and asceticism that characterized the attitudes of early church fathers. Following the rules on sexual relations, attitudes and activities of a bygone era to formulate modern religious doctrine is impractical.

Christian teaching about the limits and purposes of human sexuality is increasingly incomprehensible to a growing number of young people. The Biblical directive to "go forth and multiply" implies reproductive maximization yet the Church cautions sexual restraint? Catholic prelates have a distorted view of sex and its role in human affairs. In hindsight, one wonders if God might better have fabricated genderless creatures or at least not designed women with monthly estrus and men who are perpetually interested.

Christianity was still forming during feudal times and that legacy has survived to modern times and is visible in Church doctrine. The Christian faith is an anachronism, with social policies concerning sex and marriage that reflect the thinking of primitive minds. It is inexplicable why so much credence has been given to the writings of ancient scribes who had limited knowledge of how the world worked. Reliance on the verity of these documents is baffling. The Catholic Church is out of sync with modernity, firmly ensconced in an ancient era and very diligent in protecting its archaic doctrines. If early Christians could somehow be transported to the 21st century, they would encounter a modern world beyond their recognition and be stunned by the advances that science has made. However, they would have no problem recognizing the core doctrines of Christianity that have not changed in over 2,000 years.

The Church is a vestige of medieval thinking, endowed and enamored with ancient, outmoded biblical covenants. It needs a jolt of relevance to become meaningful in the lives of modern humans. "The big picture encompassing Western civilization during the medieval period was the cosmic universe of the Christian myth. The earth centered the heavenly spheres that traced the orbs, and the transcendent god authorized the church to preside over the dispensation of divine power and the piety it called for among nations." (Mack)

The Catholic Church has always been assertive in describing itself in as authoritative and exclusionary.

> "Certainly, the traditional vertical Church, authoritatively teaching its myth with its overwhelming majority of membership in a state of intellectual and spiritual tutelage, occupied a most ambiguous position with regard to maturation. Certainly, its hierarchical system and the kind of understanding of obedience it involved can — not alone among institutional structures, it is true — be described in some ways institutionalizing immaturity through its forms of dependence." (O'Dea)

For one hundred generations, the Western world has embraced the doctrines of Christianity as a consoling instrumentality to cope with the vicissitudes of life on Earth. The Catholic Church has always prided itself as an unchanging monolith, upholding divine promises against heretics and dissident movements. Catholicism believes it is the one true church and that "*extra Ecclesain nulla salus*," (outside the church there is no salvation.)

"Intolerance is . . . intrinsic to every creed. While all faiths have been touched, here and there, by the spirit of ecumenicalism, the central tenet of every religious tradition is that all others are mere repositories of error or, at best, dangerously incomplete." (Harris)

Scripture is often contradictory, redeeming some and punishing others. A punitive God demands unequivocal allegiance and non-believers are doomed to a fiery end. "If a man abide not in me, he is cast forth as a branch, and is withered; and men gather them, and cast them into the fire, and they are burned." (Jesus speaking in John 15:6)

"In flaming fire taking vengeance on them that know not God, and that obey not the gospel of our Lord Jesus Christ, who shall be punished with everlasting destruction from the presence of the Lord, and from the glory of his power." (Paul writing in 2 Thessalonians 1:8-9)

Religion triggers a strange human emotion. It is significantly dependent on the gullibility of its audience. Religion is a covenant with an unknown deity — a compact with an ideology. Many were born into religion, don't remember the agreement and never requested it. Traditional initiation to Christianity is usually accomplished with a dash of water splashed on one's head. There is no written contract, no handshake with God.

For a religion to flourish, two prerequisites are essential: a religious illusionist with an attractive story and a gathering of enraptured listeners. This was the environment in Palestine at the beginning of Christianity. Apocalyptic rhetoric by ecclesiastical authorities obscures observation, common sense and reason. Unfortunately, the paradox of pious ideals and the dark reality of Christian history adds a crippling degree of confusion and ambiguity to the core doctrines of Christianity.

The modern era is unconnected and distinct from the first century intellectually, economically, geographically, politically and scientifically. There is a staggering differentiation in any metric you chose. Any comparison with that era in history and the present is dubious and irrelevant. ❧

# CHAPTER THREE
# The Bible: Fact or Fabrication?

**It is virtually** impossible that what we read in the Bible today accurately corresponds with the original judgements, beliefs and teachings of Jesus. The verbiage of modern English Bibles began as oral histories of illiterate people and underwent numerous edits, revisions and translations across several languages, including Hebrew, Aramaic, Greek, Latin, German, Old English and modern English — American and British — not to mention the hundreds of other languages it has been translated into.

The Bible is the best-selling, most influential book in history, universally recognized, sporadically read and vaguely understood. It is a beguiling treatise of historical insights, partial truths, dogmatic pronouncements, puzzling parables and incomprehensible assertions. Reading and interpreting the meandering, confusing and whimsical narrative of the Good Book is a serious and challenging intellectual exercise. Yet, it is the sacred text used to authenticate Christianity, allegedly containing the words and instructions of God.

The Old Testament is the oral tradition of the Jewish people, captured in the written Hebrew language after centuries of generational interpretation. The New Testament is a metaphysical interpretation of Aramaic oral histories of Jesus and his apostles, translated into written Greek, the lingua franca of the educated of that day. Some of it is historically correct, particularly regarding Jewish customs and traditions, but much of it is puzzling to a modern reader.

If you read the Bible as history, you will be misinformed and frustrated; if you read the Bible as Christian theology you will be confused and disappointed; if you read the Bible as myth you will discover the imaginative origins of the folklore of Christian spirituality.

The lack of records written by Jesus and his disciples freed early writers of Christianity to interpret the oral histories handed down from those who knew Jesus with their own ideas and notions. The gospels were written many years after Jesus' death and the writers were not eye witnesses to the events of his life. "Most of what is written in the gospels is written based on memories of Jesus and interpretations of those memories, which had been passed along orally from persons to person for decades." (DeConick)

Literacy was uncommon in the era of Jesus. Corresponding memories of observers to an event may not be a precise rendition of what they saw or heard. It is well known that oral histories can be notoriously inaccurate and unreliable. Primitive, uneducated cultures had limited vocabularies and difficulty expressing abstract ideas. They relied on things they observed, the pragmatics of reality as they experienced it. The recollections of these people, handed down orally as stories, were interpreted and altered again by scribes writing down those memories.

Often, we read in scripture that the apostles were confused by Jesus' parables. It is unlikely these parables, confusing even when first told, were accurately conveyed by witnesses and precisely reduced to writing. One wonders if Jesus even spoke in parables or were they the fabrications of gospel writers? It seems strange that Jesus would try to convey a complex spiritual message to an illiterate audience using confusing allegories.

These oral recollections were further corrupted by translation from Aramaic to Greek, where they were edited and copied and edited again. The resulting transcriptions should be read and interpreted with caution. Since we have no access to the mind and motives of Jesus — or any Biblical characters for that matter — we are left with the mindsets and motives of male Biblical writers and their agendas.

Genesis, a complex book of the Old Testament, documents the oral history of the thoughts, experiences and beliefs of a people living in antiquity. It is believed by some to have been written by Moses, who is a legendary, not historical, figure. Most biblical scholars believe it is the work of several authors.

We have a written history of the roots of Christianity that lacks a female perspective. The quills, ink and parchment used to record random oral histories of the teachings of Jesus were controlled by men with a Greek mindset, leaving us with a prejudiced masculine view of early Christianity. The divine is obscured by a lack of empirical evidence of its existence. For all practical purposes, the original messages of Jesus are irrecoverable. Consequently, we have the challenge of interpreting early Christianity on our own terms. If we understand that memories are grossly fallible and notably deteriorate over time, we are clearly limited in our comprehension of the oral histories that were used to create the Bible.

Translators act as the bridge between cultures but word for word translations are almost never exact and a completely faithful translation is nearly impossible. A dearth of verifiable sources makes any interpretation of Biblical passages problematic. The material available to Biblical writers was anecdotal and orally transmitted by fickle memories. The multiple interpretations of New Testament Bible stories produced a final document that is almost certainly not the original word of Jesus or faithful to his true meaning.

It is a nearly impossible endeavor to succinctly capture the original thoughts, intent and words of Jesus of Nazareth. Therefore, he will forever remain an obscured figure, historically unreachable through biblical readings. The mystical, supernatural nature of many Bible passages, added to the uncertainty of events being recorded, illustrates the hopeless task of using the Bible as an accurate historical document.

"Thus, we possess no historical documents concerning those specific events in which God's revelation took place — if at all — in the form of historical facts; that is, we possess no historical documents concerning Jesus' public ministry. What we do have is simply recollections, which are always at the same time confessional in nature since in presupposition and intention they always witness to something which lies beyond mere historical factuality — something which we call revelation or salvation." (Kahler)

There are meaningful passages in the Bible, but we don't really know if they are revelations from God, utterances of Jesus or the musings of scribes. The Bible does not have a seamless voice or a consistent narrative but rather possesses a cacophony of disparate voices. Although the Bible refers to humans — and Hebrew humans in particular — as the "chosen people," the longevity spectrum among living organisms shows that trees, whales, turtles and tortoises have longer lifespans!

Scripture is universally cited by Christians as an appropriate framework for leading a religious life, but it fails to offer any guidance on modern problems. The Bible makes no mention of nuclear war, climate change, artificial intelligence, over-population, modern famine or ecological ruin. "The Christian myth and social formation (church and empire) no longer work to integrate the social interests of the modern nation-state or to solve the political issues that have developed among the modern nations-states in confrontations with the nations of the globe." (Mack)

Believing the Bible can literally be hazardous to your health. A classic example is the attrition rate among Appalachian snake handlers, who take literally Mark 16:18: "They will pick up serpents and if they drink any deadly thing, it will not harm them." Their belief that they are immune from snake bites is contradicted by the number of practitioners who die from the practice. Julia Duin, Wall Street Journal correspondent, writes in the July 13, 2018 issue that about 125 churches around Appalachia engage in the snake handling practice, During her association with those believers, two of the people she interviewed died. According to her, "Both men knew the costs of refusing medical treatment for the venom, but they believed either God would heal them — they'd survived numerous attacks before — or it was their time to die."

This is but one vivid example of a literal interpretation of the Bible that doesn't make any sense. "In the study of Scripture, ... it has become clear to the present generation of biblical scholarship, whether liberal or conservative, that the bible cannot be understood outside some historical context." (Ferguson)

"The power of written records reached its apogee with the appearance of holy scriptures. Priests and scribes in ancient civilizations became accustomed to seeing documents as guidebooks for reality. Even when scriptures mislead people about the true nature of reality, they can nevertheless retain their authority for thousands of years. The Bible peddled a monotheistic theory of history, claiming that the world is governed by a single all-powerful deity, who cares above all else about me and my doings. If something good happens, it must be a reward for my good deeds. Any catastrophe must surely be punishment for my sins." (Harari).

There is a considerable variance in belief between Catholics and Protestants on the Bible's role in the pursuit of salvation. Protestants are confident that belief in scripture, *sola scriptura*, is sufficient in itself to warrant salvation. Catholics, on the other hand, believe that belief alone is insufficient and good works are also necessary to achieve salvation. The Bible contains sufficient contradictory information that almost any interpretation can be justified by one verse or another. ❧

# A CHURCH IN PERIL

# CHAPTER FOUR
# Science Versus Religion

**Religion is not** a threat to science, but science is threating to religion. Science is religion's primary antagonist — it values proof over parables, fact over fables. It is a vital force in society and unequivocally the most effective tool for demystifying religious claims. It explains natural phenomena in understandable, empirical, observable examples. Religion makes its claims in ethereal, supernatural, existential language. In the search for truth about how the world works, science is often cited as the objective arbitrator on the differences between factual truth and moral or supernatural truth. Religious doctrines are unsupported by logic and unconnected to evidence.

Wilber, an American writer, compares science and religion:

"Fact and meaning, truth and wisdom, science and religion. It
is a strange and grotesque coexistence, with value-free science and
value-laden religion, deeply distrustful of each other, aggressively

attempting to colonize the same small planet. It is a clash of titans, to be sure, yet neither seems strong enough to prevail decisively nor graceful enough to bow out altogether. The trial of Galileo is repeated countless times, moment to moment, around the world, and it is tearing humanity, more or less, in half."

We are significantly more informed than our ancient ancestors about the natural events that occur in our world. Science significantly improves our understanding of the world and eliminates the need to seek supernatural explanations for how the world functions. There is a lot we know about the universe and life here on earth thanks to science, and still a lot we don't know.

Our current state of knowledge explains much about the universe and helps unravel the mysteries of religion and its supernatural claims. Christian cosmology originally viewed Earth as flat and the center of the universe with the sun circling the Earth. Science has since corrected that erroneous belief. The ultimate act of creation still remains a puzzle, but it is indisputable that we know absolutely nothing certain about the supernatural. By definition, the spiritual world is unknowable to the human mind. It exceeds the upper limits of our imagination. We have been told by prophets over the years that there is a God who awaits our arrival when we die, but none of their prophecies have been confirmed. Their sense of an otherworldly existence is only a figment of colorful imaginations.

"…science cannot dispel religion — not least because religion is not a set of hypotheses to be disproven. Rather, it is anything — myths, rituals, even illusions — that makes sense of our passage through life." (Scialabba)

"In religion in particular, it has often been claimed that individual religious experience is sufficient evidence for the existence of a divine or sacred reality." (Barnes)

Reason is suppressed among the religious faithful with a myriad of senseless traditions, myths, liturgies, sacraments and solemn celebratory commemorations. In my book, *All Fish Have Bones: A Recovering Catholic's Advice on Living a Good Life Without Religion* (2017), I write that the existence of the universe and humankind can be plausibly explained with science and no divine intervention was necessary. Science has its limitations, but it still remains the best objective approach we have to answer questions about how the universe works.

History is replete with misunderstandings and wrong interpretations of natural events by non-scientific observers. Prior to the introduction of objective science, religious authorities were considered the primary repositories of wisdom. In primitive cultures, religion was the explanatory trope for mysterious natural events in the world. As science gained a foothold among the educated, it began differentiating between mystery and fact, imagination and evidence.

There are essentially three frameworks for examining the world: Science, religion and our own observations and imaginations. Science and religion are firmly anchored at opposite ends of the arc of reason. Both make claims about truth. "But so far in history only the kind of careful empirical testing used by science has been shown to be a reliably effective method for determining which truth-claims are actually most probably correct and which are not, and in precisely which aspects." (Barnes)

The difficulty with religious claims about truth is that the claims are usually contaminated or distorted by bias or cultural exposure. Religion is constrained by emotional involvement and appeal to the supernatural. Science eliminates these distortions by public testing, transparency and the ability to duplicate experiments.

Science and religion are incompatible because it is impossible to study or analyze transcendental or mystical concepts. Religion is the clash of two opposing domains: the supernatural and reality. Religious belief has a vertical dimension, a sense of imaginary cosmic wonder while secular belief has a horizontal dimension; a visible, authentic, natural landscape. Religion is an example of cultural fantasy — a result of human endurance, imagination and speculative imagery.

Science, on the other hand, offers penetrating explanations of how the world works. Science dismantles much of religious doctrine, using the metric of evidence. Science provides a true understanding of nature and reality. With science there is certainty and a clarity of findings in sharp contrast to the ambiguous claims of religion.

# A CHURCH IN PERIL

Science may be unable to explicitly dispel religious claims and divine revelations because religion does not offer a testable hypothesis that can be proven or disproven. There is no reality in the supernatural and therefore nothing for scientists to see, feel, test or observe. The "spirit" world is inaccessible to measurement by scientific instruments. Science can, however, render implausible the myths, claims, revelations and illusions of religion with rigor and authority.

Hopefully, intelligent readers have determined that bad weather and misfortune in one's life are random events and not caused by a whimsical God. Religious believers have a choice to make — continue to believe in mysterious, unprovable phenomena or concede that science has the capability to distinguish between imagination and fact.

"One option is to evade, attack, reject, or vilify the method of science in order to safeguard traditional religious belief. The other option is to acknowledge the power of that method to discriminate well between truth-claims that work reliably and universally and those that do not. Only the second option is consistent with the actual history and success of science." (Barnes)

One sobering reality of the science versus religion argument is found when we examine the contributions of each to the modern world we enjoy. Our contemporary world has witnessed epic changes brought about by science, medicine, technology, philosophy and industry. We have jet airplanes, the internet, electricity, refrigeration, cell phones, television, trains and cars — all products of scientific human endeavor. From religion, we have acquired guilt, anxiety and belief in a fantasy.

Science is threatening to religion and many believers have an unfortunate and fundamental distrust of science and a troubling paranoia about the scientific community, which is perceived as the enemy of religion. Critics of science often present arguments that have a superficial appeal to those unfamiliar with the practices of science. Astrophysicist Neil DeGrasse Tyson places science in the proper perspective: "The good thing about science is that it is true whether or not you believe it."

Bloom and Skolnick Weisberg, writing in *Science*, 316 (2007), emphasize that some resistance to scientific ideas is universal: "The main reason people resist certain scientific findings then, is that many of these findings are unnatural and unintuitive. . . data suggest resistance to science will arise in children when scientific claims clash with early emerging, intuitive experiences." The concepts of evolutionary biology ". . . clash with intuitive beliefs about the immaterial nature of the soul and the purposeful design of humans and animals."

Intelligent Design (ID) advocates eschew science. They steadfastly believe in the literal Biblical version of creation — God created the world in six days and rested on the seventh. These science deniers, immune to enlightened science discoveries, have even erected a monument in Petersburg, Kentucky to reinforce their pseudoscientific beliefs. Their creationist theme park has a bogus narrative and a representation of Noah's Ark containing dioramas depicting humans living among dinosaurs.

ID proponents don't believe in evolution and focus on the dubious concept of irreducible complexity to argue their case. They typically cite the human eye as being too incredibly complicated to have accidently evolved — totally ignoring Darwin's nearly universally accepted concept that organisms evolve incrementally over exceptionally long periods of time. "God of the Gaps" is used by ID supporters to explain those spaces in longitudinal fossil records that have yet to be discovered. If science can't explain it, God did it! Their views concerning the origins of the universe and humans are an utterly and intractably opposed to reason. For ID champions, facts have become mutable.

Gottlieb's article in *Free Inquiry*, "Science vs. Religion" (February/March 2019, Vol.39, #2), points out the problems science has with testing the basic dogma of religion. "The primary assumption in Western religions is that there exists a god that is endowed with certain powers. There is no way of testing the truth of that assumption — it cannot be measured, quantified, verified, or falsified. Nor can any deductions be derived therefrom, including the made-up supernatural world associated with a god."

"Religious doctrines and institutions predate the growth of modern science. Christianity, Judaism, Islam, Hinduism, Buddhism and other religious traditions have deep roots in human history — sacred books; revered teachers and saints; the majesty of the arts; resplendent cathedrals, temples, and mosques; and deep philosophical traditions are imbued with a cultural heritage that emphasizes the need for faith and devotion. These religious institutions are ingrained in the very fabric of human civilization — its languages, concepts, and values; they define who and what we are. Indeed, they are among the oldest institutions in human history, enduring constant challenges to their hegemony. Religious prophets have been deified for what they promise. They offer meaning and purpose to life and promises of eternal salvation from this vale of tears. They are based on supernatural sources outside of nature. Science, it is claimed, deals with nature, but the divine reality transcends this in every way and beyond space and time." (Kurtz)

The opposite of the supernatural is the ordinary. We live in the ordinary, the reality of conventional existence. However, many humans inhabit two worlds: the real, tangible everyday world and an imaginary, supernatural future world. We know one is physical and real, but we can only speculate that the other mythological world exists. One we can intellectually grasp — one we can only imagine. The supernatural version of the world is narrated in the Bible — and other religious texts. The secular version is the result of scientific discoveries. Faith is suggested as the necessary agency to comprehend the supernatural.

At this time in our history, I am persuaded that religion is a rival to climate change as the greatest threat humanity has faced. Many religious people are in denial there is a problem. However, science has portrayed the threat of climate change, that, if left unaddressed, will eventually make the Earth uninhabitable. Religion is also causing untold misery with divisive groups claiming their god is greater than other gods and their followers willing to go to war to enforce their view. Religious beliefs interfere with social and political innovation due to the inability of different factions to compromise their positions. The bitter divide between religions stands in the way of hope for a peaceful planet and reconciliation among nations and cultures.

Even the U.S. does not have an enlightened intellectual majority population familiar with scientific concepts and ideas. Unfortunately, it is quite the contrary. Scientific literacy is not valued by the masses and the idea that faith trumps all evidence is illustrated by literal interpretations of Bible passages, even though most are contradicted by scientific conclusions.

The "information deficit model" predicts that as the public becomes better educated, scientific literacy would improve. This has not proven to be the case. Humans have a puzzling capacity to ignore reason when they are promised something potentially delightful — like winning the lottery or going to Heaven.

Faith is defined as the acceptance of something as true even though there is a lack of evidence or even contradictory evidence disputing the verity of the assertion. Science, on the other hand, offers a value-free, objective view of what is true, not what should be or what is desirable or undesirable. Religion purports to offer meaning, value and significance to our lives, yet it requires abundant faith in the unknown. ♦

# A CHURCH IN PERIL

# CHAPTER FIVE
# The Universe:
# Accident or Planned?

**Is human life** and the universe an accident of nature or the result of a divine hand?

There are essentially two options to explain the existence of the universe and its occupants: either a divine hand is at work or they are an accidental creation made possible by the natural laws of chemistry, physics and biology. Both are exceedingly complex ideas — hard to grasp and fully understand — but only one is true.

If you chose the divine hand option, it becomes necessary to try to determine the origin of the entity whose hand it is and how that entity became brilliant and knowledgeable enough to create the complexities of all creatures on earth. The accidental option only requires belief in evolution, the theory that living organisms come into existence over long periods of time via favorable mutation, differential reproduction and natural selection for survival traits.

Both scenarios are difficult to envision. The solution is to pick the explanation that is most reasonable, sensible and feasible, the one most clearly described and supported by the best evidence.

I favor the explanation that is logical, persuasive, plausible, consistent with the laws of nature and doesn't require supernatural intervention. The Catholic Church does allow belief in evolution as long as God is inserted somewhere in the process, but evolution offers a better explanation for the random makeup of the natural word than the creation myth in Genesis.

Studying the origin of the universe and the existence of humans and the other organisms on Earth is challenging. Stephen Jay Gould (1941-2002), a famous Harvard paleontologist, believed that if the evolutionary tape was rewound and run again, humans might not be one of the results. Human beings are a highly unlikely phenomenon and bewildering to comprehend, but we happened.

It is exceeding difficult to comprehend that the diversity among the Earth's flora and fauna arose as evolutionary accidents. It is equally challenging to imagine that a divine cosmic force in the sky with a gigantic brain designed and created that diversity we enjoy.

When intelligent individuals look at their surroundings, most are awe struck at the grandeur, beauty and diversity of the living organisms on the planet. Elephants and squirrels, pine trees and orchids, eagles and hummingbirds, mosquitoes and spiders, birds and fish and cats and dogs all live in one ecosystem. When one sees a Monarch butterfly perched on the back of an African bush elephant, bumblebees using long hairy tongues to suck nectar from a dinner-plate-sized dahlia, peacocks displaying their iridescent tail feathers, the delicacy of a tropical orchid or the majesty of a towering Ponderosa pine, one can't help but be astonished — and confused — at the enormous variety and beauty of plants, insects and animals on planet Earth and wonder how they came into existence.

The natural world surrounding us is unfathomably complex. The tremendous diversity in flora and fauna tends to exceed comprehension by a scientifically unsophisticated population. People are unable to understand nature, define it or grasp its origin and evolution. They seem unable to comprehend the mechanism of evolution.

Geologist Marcia Bjornerud believes, "As a species, we have a childlike disinterest in the time before our appearance on Earth . . . resistance to the concept of evolution is rooted more in existential dread than in religious doctrine, and that it declines as people become more familiar with stories from the natural world." For her, geology is a way to see our past by studying rocks, landscapes, groundwater, glaciers and ecosystems, and that can help us find a way to the future. "Geology points to a middle way between narcissistic pride in our importance and existential despair at our insignificance."

In 1940, folksinger Woody Guthrie wrote the song *This Land is Your Land, This Land is My Land*. The ending line of the chorus is, "This land was made for you and me." Sorry Woody, you were wrong. This land wasn't made for us. It was naturally formed over eons by a combination of incredibly slow evolution and a series of cataclysmic events that shaped and continues to shape the planet we call home.

Look around wherever you live. Chances are there is some form of devastation or landscape change occurring. As I write, a volcano is erupting on an island close to where I live, forest fires are raging in California, flooding is occurring in the Midwest, tsunamis constantly menace world coastlines and global warming threatens the planet itself. Close observation of the planet shows it is a dangerous place for humans to live and certainly not "made for you and me!"

The claim in Genesis that the planet was deliberately constructed by a brilliant invisible architect seems unlikely. Earthlings live on earthquake fault lines; in tsunami zones, tornado and hurricane alleys; on flood plains and snow and ice-covered tundra. Humans search for suitable living space in a mosaicked landscape created by the migration of tectonic plates sliding unpredictably around on the Earth's surface, sometimes causing immense damage and loss of life. The entire human population literally resides on shaky ground.

God is portrayed by religion as the benevolent, all powerful Creator, the intelligent Designer of the universe and everything in it. But close inspection of His work exposes some significant flaws. As a designer, God failed miserably in the areas of ecology, human anatomy and planet construction.

- Seventy percent of Earth is covered with non-potable salt water. Only 30 percent remains for His land-based "chosen" creatures — and both poles of the Earth are ice covered year-round.
- The Earth is a dangerous place to live. Earthquakes, volcanoes, tsunamis, tornados, floods and hurricanes regularly cause physical destruction and loss of human life.
- The anatomy of the human body has numerous flaws with unnecessary organs and faulty nerve and blood pathways.
- Mosquitoes appear to have no value except to annoy and spread disease. At the Bill and Melinda Gates Foundation Discovery Center in Seattle, an exhibition reveals that 725,000 people die every year from mosquito-borne diseases.
- Animals have to kill and eat each other to survive.
- Humans suffer from numerous serious illnesses.
- Trees and some animals enjoy longer life spans than humans.
- There have been five mass extinctions since the Earth was formed, significantly decreasing the biodiversity on Earth.

I believe these imperfections and aberrations are compelling indicators that the formation of the Earth and its inhabitants was the result of natural causes and not a divine hand!

Since recorded history began about 5,000 years ago, humans in the Western world have held an exalted view of their place in the universe. Religion encourages humans in their troubling conviction of their superiority over other organisms in nature. The erroneous belief that humans are special creations and the Earth is the center of the universe was debunked by the discoveries of Galileo and Darwinian evolution. This should not be viewed as a depressing situation but rather an awaking to the value of the life we have and our proper place in the cosmos where we live.

Pulitzer Prize-winning writer and Harvard biologist Edward O. Wilson writes in his best-selling book, *The Social Conquest of Earth*, "Our lives are restrained by two laws of biology: all of life's entities and processes are obedient to the laws of physics and chemistry; and all of life's entities and processes have arisen through evolution by natural selection."

Humans themselves are changing the natural world rapidly. So rapidly in fact, that scientists have given our epoch the name Anthropocene — the "human age." Our challenge is to discover what can be done about the rapid degradation of the planet so the natural world will still be around for our children and grandchildren. We should accept and grieve for what has vanished forever, but devote our energies to understanding our mistakes and how best to insure they are not repeated.

"The world is not an optional investment we can choose to forgo due to its low rate of return. There is no Planet B. We have to keep this planet healthy, because it's our only one and only home, our extended body." (Robinson) ❧

# A CHURCH IN PERIL

# CHAPTER 6
# The Lure of Immortality

**At some point** in the future, you will die. There's no way to forecast when or how it will occur; it may happen quickly or slowly, but it will happen. It is the inevitable fate that awaits us all; the price of birth, an event we can neither avoid nor alter. The specter of death — the end of a life on earth — and the thought of existential nothingness is a difficult concept for humans to ponder and one that is impossible to sugarcoat. Death is the mother of all enigmas.

According to the Bible, mortality began with the "fall" of Adam and Eve in the Garden of Eden. Their punishment was manual labor and painful child bearing, respectively, and eventual death. Knowing there is an end to life is a frightening curse on sentient beings and one of the primary attractions of the religious promise of an afterlife. The lure of immortality is a human fascination motivated by the fear of death. You can't escape dying but you can approach it with a degree of understanding that it is a normal consequence of life.

For the religious, death is a beginning.

"Throughout history, religions and ideologies did not sanction life itself. They always sanctified something above or beyond earthy existence, and were consequently quite tolerant of death. Indeed, some of them have been downright fond of the Grim Reaper. Because Christianity, Islam and Hinduism insisted that the meaning of our existence depended on our fate in the afterlife, they viewed death as a vital and positive part of the world. Humans died because God decreed it, and their moment of death was a sacred metaphysical experience exploding with meaning." (Harari)

For the non-religious, death is the end; humans are combinations of atoms that are dispersed into the cosmos afterward for reuse in some unknown manner. We are assured by religious authorities that there is a posthumous existence, but the lack of certainty that something exists "somewhere on the other side" coupled with the finality of death observed on multiple occasions makes the event unwelcome and terrifying.

Life on Earth is not a rehearsal for a future adventure — it *is* the main event. It's fair to say that most humans desire a long, healthy, youthful-appearing, stress-free, meaningful, pleasurable life; to experience a pleasant retirement; and die peacefully, pain free and with a sense of dignity. The difficult truth is that every one of us will eventually conclude that we have reached a point where our physical decline is so obvious that it cannot be denied — or reversed. There are not many things in the world that are certain but life has a 100 percent mortality rate. Most of our lives are spent making choices designed to postpone death. We think of death as something that happens to other people, until it doesn't.

Unfortunately, neither science nor religion has been successful in assuaging our fear of dying. Our lives are consumed with an endless search for meaning, happiness and purpose. We live in a depersonalized world and many individuals who feel lost seek solace in religious organizations. The angst created by contemplating the end of our life on Earth makes the enchanting lure of immortality irresistible.

Even considering the reassurance of clerics, many in the U.S. have not achieved a comfort level with the idea of death and continue to embrace the potential of posthumous immortality. Gospel songs have been used for years by church musicians to generate acceptance of death and paint a rosy picture of the process of crossing over to the other side. But even the beloved 19th century hymn, *Nearer, My God, to Thee*, describing Jacob's dream in Genesis that has him "on joyful wing, cleaving the sky. Upwards I fly; nearer, my God, to Thee" does little to diminish our fear of death. It's a beautiful hymn but most of us are not interested in getting nearer to God anytime soon. The hymn, *How Great Thou Art*, is a classic in the gospel repertoire and my favorite, especially when sung by the ambrosial voices of the Statler brothers, with the uplifting lyrics, "When Christ will come and lead me home, what joy shall fill my heart." However, joy is not the usual emotion we express at the time of death. The inverse of the lyrics is more faithful to the usual emotions humans experience about death.

Other than the sex drive, the desire for immortality is the strongest impulse in humans — none of us want to die. But have you ever contemplated living forever and ever and ever and ever? Superficially, the idea has a fascinating attraction, but if you thoughtfully dissect the concept, it begins to lose its allure. I think most of us — after two, three or four hundred years — would become bored and begin to look forward to an end!

Although there is no metaphysical certainty for this assertion, conventional Christianity teaches that death is the beginning of eternal life. According to Catholic teaching, gravity still has a hold on your physical body when you die, but your soul is released to ascend into the cosmos to be rewarded or punished by God according to your activities on Earth. Catholic death is surrounded by an elaborate ceremony with prayers, incense, holy water and eulogies; the sacrament of *Anointing of the Sick*. This ritual has no effect on the departed but is intended to assuage the grief of the survivors.

Supposedly angels and devils fight for the soul of the departed!

Religion presents a paradoxical mixture of suffering and misery of life on Earth exchanged for happiness and bliss in an afterlife. The focus of the

Catholic Church is on the "end times" — not the anxieties of the living, not a celebration of life, not an optimistic enthusiasm for life, but the potentialities of life after death. *Memento mori* (remember that you are mortal) is the early Christian Latin expression reminding Christians of the transient nature of life on Earth. Today's youth use the acronym YOLO (you only live once).

The idea that the end of earthly life is not the end of living but a new beginning is a fascinating concept and a powerful message used to draw people to religion. This celestial abstraction, belief in salvation preached by religious clerics, is the central tenant of religion. It is a simplistic and seductive concept. There is a calming reassurance in being told that you will never die. However, it is profoundly disturbing and particularly disappointing that our Creator who gave us life, did not furnish us with the emotional tools to prepare us for death. Death is certain, salvation is conjecture. Each of us lives our own portion of eternity until it ends.

In eschatological religious liturgy, the *eschaton* (end of time) describes the drama of the end of the world when the Messiah returns and ushers in the Kingdom of God on Earth. Since that event has apparently been postponed, each of us will have to confront the completion of our own earthly existence on our own.

Death can be viewed either as a hopeless circumstance or a natural part of existence. The ancient Greek philosopher Epicurus did not fear death. In a letter to Menoeceus, a Greek mythological figure, he described his pragmatic attitude toward death and dying: "So death, the most frightening of bad things, is nothing to us; since when we exist, death is not yet present, and when death is present, then we do not exist. Therefore, it is relevant neither to the living nor to the dead, since it does not affect the former, and the latter do not exist."

The aging process is not well understood, but it's a reality we have to cope with. Growing old is generally unwelcome. Most of us would gladly postpone it if we could. As the arc of life begins its descent, there is a certain existential despair at the idea that someday our lives will be over and insignificant. An irony of dying is that you can't experience it ahead of time and make preparation. It is a one-time experience that is only realized by actually doing it. Comedian Woody Allen captured this notion in his quip, "I'm not afraid of death, I just don't want to be there when it happens."

The onset of old age is insidiously quick—one day you're young and vibrant and the next day you're suddenly decrepit and on the threshold of dying. Aging is not a condition to be solved; it is a predicament to be understood and dealt with. Aging can be approached with defiance, resentment, despair or acceptance. Attempting to reverse the aging process and master the terms of our own existence is a wasteful and futile exercise. The decline in physical and cognitive functions may be slowed down but it is unlikely they can be significantly undone. For the elderly, mortality is a daily companion, a reality to muddle through. Disease and disability are stochastic events that we cannot control.

The elderly dismiss the idea of mortality as an abstract notion as they experience their own decline, coupled with everyday reminders in the passing of friends and relatives. Attending a funeral or viewing a deceased friend is a stark jolt of reality, a periodic reminder that life is fleeting and not perpetual.

Living is actually a lengthy process of dying; a complex progression between the thresholds of birth and death, compounded by the knowledge that someday it will happen. We can look for comfort in actuary tables, but recognize those numbers are averages and individually don't have much predictive significance. Life is the remarkable intermezzo between here and not here, between beginning and ending.

The Danish philosopher Kierkegaard described aging as the "evening of life," a lyrical poetic nuance that does nothing to disguise its finality. However it is couched, it is the final chapter, the last stage of life leading to an irrevocable termination of existence on Earth, the cessation of all human function, a darkness from which there is no recovery. The idea of successful aging is undoubtedly an oxymoron, but, "Seeing our circumstances clearly requires us to ask why we regard aging and death as realities to hide, why we can't we cope with our inevitable decline, and why we can't maintain our sense of self in the face of dependency, disability, and an aging body." (Davis)

Acceptance of the inevitability of death is one of the great difficulties confronting humans. Whenever I pass a cemetery I am reminded that the only immortal things residing there are the plastic flowers adorning the graves.

Sadly, our American culture does not honor or value the elderly. They are often neglected, and their wisdom, dignity, leadership, survival skills and contributions to society are overlooked. Many are financially impoverished, lonely and with serious health issues. Once they reach an arbitrary expiration date, they are mentally consigned to the dustbin of history where they expire in isolation without supporting resources.

Many are actuarially old but physically and mentally young. They are still undervalued and not welcomed in the workforce even though many remain able-bodied and cognitively alert well into the upper age brackets. For those in pain, government intrusion — corroborated by religious institutions — denies their right to death with dignity at a time of their choosing. It's preposterous to have government — or religious — rules about when and how to die. There are limited government programs to support the elderly yet they maintain control over our departure.

Devaluing our elderly population is a shame and one of the egregious failures of the American philosophy of human value. The elderly deserve respect and admiration for their contributions to society and sympathy for their aging problems.

It seems strange that religion values an anticipated life for which there is no evidence over one that is actually experienced. Yet, many are consumed seeking the Gospel of eternal life, a journey to the Promised Land. However, if religion removed the promise of eternal life from its creed, it would have the lifespan of a mayfly!

To believe in an afterlife, one has to substitute unsubstantiated "divine revelation" for the reality of existence. Yet the dream of a better life than the one we are living is a powerful motivator that nourishes a deep yearning within us for an extension to our earthly lives. Humans have a propensity for spiritual longing. Searching for hope and meaning in the abyss of existence is a distraction from the inevitability of death. People have problems contemplating the meaning and reality of nonexistence and no interest in testing the concept.

The concept of Heaven is an enigma. What happens at the intersection of life and death is unknown, so we are free to speculate what an afterlife might look like. Is there meaning in Heaven? What will we do there? If there is nothing to do, how will you spend your time?

We can imagine what a heavenly existence ought to be: free beer, par golf, sex with anybody and a fish bite on every cast. You are limited only by your imagination. However, a sober analysis of the existence of the Christian Heaven shows it has been sparsely described — not much beyond a place where God lives. Heaven is obviously outside the confines of our planet and solar system and, to date, beyond the views of any of our powerful land-based and orbiting telescopes. Sort of like Santa's workshop.

Psalm 23:4 comforts us and tells us we should not fear death: "Yea, though I walk through the valley of the shadow of death, I will fear no evil: for thou art with me."

The allure and futility of chasing immortality is one of the great conundrums of life. If an afterlife was certain beyond doubt and supported by evidence and experience, the fear of death would miraculously disappear. But, the afterlife is only a reassuring myth. The notion that we can leave behind the trials, tribulations and painful experiences of a past life on earth and emerge in a new, beatific existence in Heaven is a religious aphrodisiac that assuages the fear of death. This concept cannot be rationally established and — with the exception of the alleged resurrection of Jesus — has never been observed or experienced. It is unsubstantiated, highly implausible, violates all the rules of nature and no examples have been witnessed in the 2,000 years since Jesus' purported rise from the dead. But even the remote possibility that it might be true is mesmerizing to religious believers.

The religious concept of life after death infiltrates into our head and rearranges the neurons. What is implausible and without evidence suddenly becomes enticingly realistic. But how many dead people do you know who have come back to life? Science has essentially nullified many of the underlying assumptions of this religious doctrine. There is no available evidence that passes scientific scrutiny and concludes there is life after death. Unfortunately, there is only death after life.

In discussions about religion and the afterlife, I have found that many people who are not particularly religious occupy an agnostic "maybe" space that they find comfortable between faith in the supernatural and reality. Like Pascal and his "wager," they are hedging their bets, reluctant to commit to an absolute position on a potential afterlife, but keeping open the possibility, however remote.

When someone we love dies, we commonly accentuate the wrong emotion. Obviously, there is an authentic physical and emotional void in our lives and the departed will be genuinely missed. It is challenging to entertain philosophical musings on life and death when mourning, but if we can be rational for a moment, we know that all lives will end in death.

Remember that death is not contagious. The end of one life does not signal the end of others. Rather than immersing ourselves in sorrow and focusing on our loss, we might instead think about the effect the departed had on our lives and remembering the joy and contentment that their unique personality brought us while they were alive. A loved one may be physically gone but their legacy of life remains with us until we depart as well. Although traumatic and depressing, the death of friends and relatives can offer unintended opportunities to reexamine our own lives, be grateful that we are still alive, and assist in adopting a renewed enthusiasm for our own living experience. ❧

# CHAPTER SEVEN
# Some Assembly Required

**It is a** foundational concept of Christianity that there is life beyond death. One of the attractions of Catholic Christianity is the expectation that bodies and souls will be miraculously reunited in Heaven. The Catholic Church teaches that human bodies — with their corresponding souls — will be resurrected and reconstituted in the hereafter. This is the concept of ensoulment — that every human being has an everlasting soul; immortal and indestructible. According to Catholic teaching, it enters your body at conception and departs for an afterlife when you die. Your body dies, but the soul continues to exist in some unknown form.

Souls are invisible and none of us has ever seen anyone return from the grave to claim theirs. We are continually reminded by preachers that we will be reassembled in heaven, but the precise details of this process are always sketchy. It remains unclear whether we will be retrofitted with the athletic body of our youth, our physique at the prime of life, or the decrepit carcass at the time of death. In my case, I would hope my prostate would be restored at the very least, although since sex in Heaven is questionable, I'm not sure of what value it might be!

For Eve's transgression in the Garden of Eden, all of humanity is condemned by God to a lifetime of servile labor and eventual death. Ashes to ashes, dust to dust — a biblical epigram originating in Genesis 3:19; "dust thou art and unto dust shalt thou return" — reminds us that we were formed from the Earth's dust and destined to end up as dust. But, converting a corpse to ashes was forbidden by the Catholic Church until 1963 when Pope Paul VI lifted the ban on cremation. His letter, *Ad Resurged Cum Christo* (Resurrection with Christ), allowed priests to officiate at cremation ceremonies. The Church still bans division of the cremains and frowns on scattering them on land or water or keeping them at home in urns. The Church recommends that ashes be buried in a cemetery or kept in a sacred place. I call this the Humpty-Dumpty problem. Evidently God, even with all His infinite power and skill, might have difficulty putting scattered or divided ashes back together again.

Religion is the closest most of us will ever come to a near-death experience. Believers are constantly reminded during church services that death is right around the corner, and in fact it may be, but continual reminders of it creates undue anxiety. Couching it as a new beginning does little to enhance its appeal. ❧

# CHAPTER EIGHT
# Pondering the Inscrutable Mystery of Faith

**It would appear** that the prophesied arrival of a savior to emancipate the world has been postponed indefinitely. The heavens have not parted, no mystical glow is evident, angels are nowhere in sight and the celestial choir must be on sabbatical. Clearly, the arrival of the Messiah is not at hand. After waiting for 2,000-plus years, one could assume that either the prophesy was made using geologic time frames or conclude that the arrival may never take place.

Since Christ's return was deferred and the Second Coming cannot be predicted, Christianity had to manufacture a plausible scenario leaving redemption still a viable concept but with an unknown timespan. Theological wizardry produced doctrines justifying the delay, but the image of Jesus as the son of God recedes further and further into the past every year, as the distance increases between the conception of Christianity and the present.

# A CHURCH IN PERIL

It may be constructive to ask questions that have not been answered, explore avenues of inquiry that have been ignored and potentially arrive at conclusions that may contradict previously cherished religious beliefs.

Religious believers can be described as the curious in pursuit of the mysterious and unexplainable. The single most important theological dogma in religion is that God exists! It is assumed in Western religions that a single God exists and that He created the universe and keeps track of all of the activities of His creations. The truth of that assumption cannot be tested or measured in any way, nor can it be denied. If God exists and is a good guy (or girl), I believe He or She would want us to employ our neuron-packed craniums He or She created and try to understand ourselves and the universe where we live.

"In answer to the question, why do people believe? The first explanation is that believers have not been exposed to the factual critiques of their faith. Accordingly, a second explanation for this is that noncognitive tendencies and impulses are at work, tempting believers to accept the 'unbelievable.' . . . Most of the classical religious beliefs emerged in a prescientific era before the application of the methods of science." (Kurtz)

"How does religion fit into a mind that one might have thought was designed to reject the palpably not true? The common answer — that people take comfort in the thought of a benevolent shepherd, a universal plan, or an afterlife — is unsatisfying, because it only raises the question of why a mind would evolve to find comfort in beliefs it can plainly see are false." (Pinker)

Christianity is noteworthy for its message's simplicity, but the creed is complicated and elusive enough in understanding to sustain numerous interpretations. It presents an ambiguous image — a primitive belief derived from an ancient, obscure, distorted vision of reality.

Christianity is currently undergoing an existential crisis. Its theology is being questioned, its relevance is waning and it is confronted with a serious question of identity. "The decline of religion in the West began with the Enlightenment. The 18th century European Enlightenment marked the first serious questioning of religious faith within Western societies, although the Church's absolute power and authority had already been partially undermined during the 16th century Protestant Reformation." (Lewis)

The legacy of early Christianity was developed from the remnants of an ancient myth that has little relevance to the modern world. According to O'Dea, "Christianity became institutionalized on the three levels of cult, belief, and organized fellowship, and this institutionalization has long provided the context for Western man's religious experience."

Devout Christians are now confronted with a schizoid world: they live in the modern era but are philosophically and theologically anchored to a mythical world of antiquity. The Catholic Church in particular has a dysfunctional nostalgia for mythical events that purportedly took place in primitive times. Catholics have become inured to the tedium of being trapped in a weekly, folkloric ritual that has long since lost any sense of meaning.

In *The Prehistory of the Mind*, Mithen reports the three recurrent features of religious ideologies cited by anthropologist Pascal Boyer in his book, *The Naturalness of Religious Ideas*:

"The first is that in many societies it is assumed that a non-physical component of a person can survive after death and remain as a being with beliefs and desires. Second, it is very frequently assumed that certain people within a society are especially likely to receive direct inspiration or messages from supernatural agencies, such as gods or spirits. And third, it is also very widely assumed that performing certain rituals in an exact way can bring about change in the natural world."

One of the great paradoxes of our century is that while we push the edge of scientific and technological envelopes, we persist in clinging with childlike enthusiasm to an archaic fairy tale of creation involving a naked lady, a snake, a fruit tree and a punitive deity. The powerful iconic image fabricated from the tale in the Garden of Eden established a framework of Christianity that has endured for centuries — sin, guilt, punishment and fear. Sin and its attendant guilt are the centerpiece of Christianity, accompanied by its corresponding relationship with forgiveness.

Sin cannot go unforgiven in the Judeo-Christian tradition, but must be discharged in some way. Forgiveness is associated with the Christian Deity, who traditionally dispenses it through His ministers on Earth.

> "In the Jewish moral world in which Christianity originated, and without which it would have been unthinkable, sin had always had to be paid for, generally by the sacrificial shedding of blood; its effects could never be ignored or willed away. Which is precisely why, in the Christian context, forgiveness of sin was specifically related to Jesus Christ's atoning sacrifice, his vicarious payment for all human sins, procured through his death on the cross and made available freely to all who embraced him in faith. Forgiveness is one of the chief antidotes to the forensic stigma of guilt, and as such has long been one of the golden words of our culture, with particularly deep roots in the Christian tradition, in which the capacity for forgiveness is seen as a central attribute of the Deity itself." (McClay)

Religion appeals to basic human emotions. It offers moral and spiritual guidance, solace during times of crisis, plus a sense of identity and belonging to something greater than ourselves. It counters the melancholia of life with promises of better things to come.

Personal religion is generally a consequence of birth, not a conscious and informed choice made by mature individuals. As we transition from adolescent innocence to mature, enlightened skepticism, the veil of mystique of religious beliefs slowly gives way to reasoning and logic. In my experience, many people — myself included — attend church and practice Catholicism but devote very little time and effort to studying and understanding thorny theological issues.

Many believers identify with a church because of its traditions, liturgy, culture and social programs rather than basic doctrinal belief. People attend church seeking exaltation, illumination and comfort, but often leave with a vague and confused notion of what the Church has to offer that will be beneficial in their lives.

Life is a continuous exercise in trying to distinguish between what is real and what is make-believe or just plain fake. Reality and religion occupy separate and distinct domains: the real world we live in and the paranormal world of spirit, God. Religion is about gods, miracles, ghosts, sin, Heaven and Hell and redemption — a fascinating juxtaposition of bleak reality with an imaginary blissful world.

Human life, on the other hand, is messy; a combination of adventure, accomplishment and disappointment. What humans experience is real life; joy and pain, eating, drinking, working, laughing and crying, raising a family and coping with the vicissitudes of life. Educated people are more interested in material things that sustain life rather than obtuse theological discussions. This is one of the reasons for the rapid advancement of secularism in developed democracies.

Mining the history of Christianity exposes the profound but understandable ignorance of early Christian believers. Their lack of education and plethora of superstitions contributed to a primitive view of the world that satisfied their concerns but was substantially incorrect. History beyond 500 years ago is difficult to accurately portray. Times have changed, written historical records are scarce and all the participants are dead. This often leads to a misrepresentation of the actual events and their proper context.

History is written by the winners, and it can suppress facts, advance agendas and introduce conspiracies. According to Shermer, 80 to 90 percent of people in medieval times were illiterate. "Most could not even read the Bible, particularly since it was written in Latin, guaranteeing that it would remain the exclusive intellectual property of an elite few. Almost everyone believed in sorcery, werewolves, hobgoblins, witchcraft, and black magic."

In the case of religion, the past has captured the present and won't let it go. One should pause and examine the claims of the three Abrahamic religions, which all assert their God is the one authentic God. Yet, each group is composed of different people, believing different things, reading different books and declaring their doctrines are truer than the others.

"All these faiths [Judaism, Christianity and Islam] though
shrouded in mystery, claim divine sanctification. There are
certain common features which each of these religion manifests
— historic claims of revelations by charismatic prophets
promising eternal salvation; sacred books detailing their
miraculous prophecies, prescribing rituals, prayers, and rites
of passage; a priestly class which seeks to enforce religious law;
great temples, cathedrals, and mosques where the Lord is present
in the mysteries of the sacraments." (Kurtz)

Oppressed cultures are vulnerable to any expression or narrative that
promises to improve their lives. They want to believe.

"When social conditions include oppression of a people,
there is a good chance that the response will be the belief in a
rescuing messiah delivering redemption. The messiah myth,
like all myths, may be a fictitious narrative, but it represents
something deeply nonfictional about human nature and human
history. To this extent it is an important component in answer to
the question of how we believe." (Shermer)

Religion is intrusive in our lives. It established rules and traditions to be
followed. It introduces discomfort that we patiently endure in exchange for a
promised eternal salvation. Religion offers a structural framework for life —
traditions, rituals and prayers to help cope with the vicissitudes of living — a
self-help program for coping with the miseries of everyday living. The pomp
and circumstance attendant to the practice of religion tend to mask the flaws
in the fundamental doctrines.

"Historically, Catholicism has spelled out a complex of answers,
embodied them in its creed and liturgies, and built around them
its communal and hierarchical structure. This set of themes,
institutionalized within the Church, provided the basic answers to
Western man's problem of meaning for centuries. The answers were
guaranteed and underwritten by the sense of the immediacy and
reality of God and of man's relationship to him and participation

with him in the Church which long characterized Catholic faith
and remains its greatest source of strength." (O'Dea)

Religion is a mythical trope that purports to answer basic human questions:

"Who am I?"

"Where did I come from?"

"Where am I going?"

"Will I have another life after my earthly existence?"

However, these question continue to go unanswered and remain a church mystery.

"In his allocution to the opening of the second session of the [Second Vatican) Council, Pope Paul VI declared: 'The Church is a mystery. It is a reality imbued with the hidden presence of God.'" (O'Dea)

Religion is ingenious. It doesn't replace truth with fiction — it wraps fiction with a veneer of reality. Crafty theologians try to convince religious believers that fiction is fact, that the supernatural is reality and fairytales and myth are authentic history. The exaggerated exhortations of zealous prelates defending antiquated theology does not make it true. Theologians, with their torturous logic and ideological delusions, can twist mythology into what appears to be reality. The paradox of religion is that its doctrines are obviously bogus, yet they are compelling.

Religion has a dark, apocalyptic motif that contradicts its message of love and good will. The accretion of centuries of ecclesiastical rules and regulations has all but buried the original message of love and compassion preached by Jesus of Nazareth. An anthropologist would be challenged today to uncover the preaching of Jesus in the trappings and traditions that have morphed into modern Christianity. Religion devalues the very life we are living — choosing instead to focus on an ethereal, problematic afterlife. Catholic religion fails to deliver the love, warmth, support and encouragement sought by the faithful to aide in coping with life on Earth. Little empathy is expressed by priests who act as disciplinarians and life referees, enforcing rigid rules and regulations purported to guide the faithful on the journey toward salvation. For all of its concentration on love and goodness, it has an ominous, tragic spirit of doom.

# A CHURCH IN PERIL

Religious history from preliterate times to the advent of Judeo-Christianity is a journey from a mélange of gods to a Supreme God. The idea of a single God responsible for the universe and all its contents is novel, provocative and relatively new. The three great monotheistic religions, Judaism (4,000 years), Christianity (2,000 years) and Islam (1,300 years) proclaim there is only one unique, supreme creator and moral leader of the universe. Polytheism, on the other hand — as old as superstition — tolerates many gods, each with their own capabilities and spheres of influence. Combining all the gods of history with their diverse powers and attributes is innovative and tidy but results in a complex persona with immense responsibility.

The common notion of a supernatural God is a cognitively difficult illusion to grasp — a vague and ethereal abstraction that defies reality or possibility of discovery. One may ask, is monotheism an improvement over polytheism? What is gained by paying homage to one God instead of many gods? Polytheism seems more intuitively logical, with each god specializing in one area and supplicants directing their worries and apprehensions to a particular god for relief.

Neither polytheism nor monotheism have been successful at answering the basic questions of the beginning of the universe and the creation of Earth and its inhabitants. It appears that morality can be achieved by believing in either one god or many.

"Monotheism achieves this result [morality] by denying reality to all gods but one and then ascribing to that one god a supreme concern with morality. Polytheism typically achieves the same result by denying supreme importance to any of the gods, however many they may be, and assigning it instead to an impersonal necessity of some kind whose workings favor and enforce morality and affect gods and men alike." (Miles)

Evolutionary morality suggests people behave in a moral manner without expectation of reward or punishment because it simply makes sense to cooperate with fellow humans. Harari claims, "From an ethical perspective, monotheism was arguably one of the worst ideas in human history. What monotheism did was to make many people far more intolerant than before . . . the late Roman

Empire was as diverse as Ashoka's[1] India, but when Christianity took over, the emperors adopted a very different approach to religion."

Christianity has an illogical and contradictory identity. It is both a remarkable success and a terrifying tragedy. Both positive and negative attributes thrive under the umbrella of Christianity. From a humble beginning, Christianity morphed into a stunning religious sensation now attracting billions of followers all over the world. It also has been used as justification for barbaric acts of violence against humanity by religious and political leaders and individuals.

This bifurcated personality of Christianity is manifested in the way we interpret our God. Monotheism focused our attention on a single god, but if we look closely we have either two gods or one god with a split personality. One of our gods is a pious god, a kind, compassionate, forgiving and supporting god. The other god is an angry god, a mercurial, vengeful god who smites enemies, exacts revenge and punishes the unfaithful.

This schizophrenic god defies rational understanding due to its mystical nature. The exotic terrain of the supernatural, by definition, is beyond the reach of language — beyond the power of words to convey a plausible image. The human dilemma of trying to grasp the concept of the supernatural requires leaving the comforts of certainty and treading cautiously in the land of the unknown.

The supernatural cannot be accurately described — or predicted — since it cannot be observed. Nor can it be proven to exist by using current scientific methods. It is simply beyond our understanding. Therefore, we humans are forced to use simplistic metaphors to explain our imaginations of the supernatural; restrained by the forces of gravity, stuck on Earth, trying to describe a kingdom in the sky.

The Christian God is presented as a cosmic expression with three personas: supernatural being, human being in the person of Jesus, and omnipresent spirit. But, the traditional attributes assigned to God are not necessarily

---

[1]Ashoka the Great was an Indian emperor of the Maurya Dynasty, who ruled the Indian subcontinent from ca 268 to 232 BCE.

accurate. We have a god of goodness competing for human attention with a despotic god. The virtuous characteristics are the ones we hope God has but they may not be the ones God actually has or feels are necessary for His work.

Humans reside in a material universe that is substantially explained by science and, as nearly as we can tell, independent of any supernatural sustaining force. For intelligent humans, reality is all there is. Most of our imagery of God, Heaven and Hell come from drawings and paintings, the results of the imaginations of human artists. If realities exist beyond our imaginations and insights, they will continue to remain suppressed and mysterious until explained by a visiting supernatural force. If an alternate universe does exist, it is unknown to the human mind and therefore irrelevant.

Religion functions in the nebulous arenas of speculation, promise and faith. Religion is the product of superstition, imagination, myth, and the delusions of prophets. "Its main function is to overcome despair and hopelessness in response to human tragedy, adversity and conflict — the brute inexplicable, contingent, and fragile aspects of the human condition." (Kurtz)

However, there is an interesting relationship between faith and doubt. Doubt is a subset of the idea of faith and since faith deals with the unknown, doubt is an important component of the faith mindset. Religious faith ignores logic and reason and requires reliance on divine revelation to ascertain the "truth." The "truth" of mysteries of faith is hidden and only arrived at through belief in divine revelation, while secular reality is arrived at by natural reasoning. Reason and faith are mutually exclusive: you cannot employ reason to understand faith.

The acceptance of ancient dogmas at face value, without any analysis or inquiry into their origin, verity or rationality is astonishing to me. However, I was guilty of this for many years, assuming that religious authorities were smarter than I about theology and that they had rational foundations for their teachings. I have since learned that theology is a dead-end academic discipline. Trying to explain unknown unknowns is a pointless exercise.

Catholic dogma has been exposed to the elements for over 2,000 years and has developed a rusty patina. Times change, norms change, discoveries enlighten, concepts evolve and the human species becomes more sophisticated. Religion, however, seems to have acquired rigor mortis. Blind acceptance in the 21st century of an idea crafted in a primitive era to deal with superstition represents a dysfunctional nostalgia for archaic dogma. President Lincoln recognized the folly of applying ancient beliefs to solve modern problems. In his annual message to Congress in 1862 he said, "The dogmas of the quiet past are inadequate to the stormy present."

One of the puzzling things about Christianity is that its bedrock doctrines are based on ancient fantasies with no real connection to any historical reality. When searching for insights into the mysteries of religion, one encounters a "nothingness" component — the nonexistence of much of what is claimed to be real.

Religion preaches three great untruths:

If you live a good life on earth, when you die you will go to another place and be happy forever. If you were bad, you will be eternally punished in everlasting fire.

You were conceived in sin and are prone to be a sinner.

God loves you.

The reality is that you were not conceived in sin; are not prone to sin; will not go anyplace when you die; and since God doesn't exist, He can't very well love you, and if He does exist He apparently doesn't care.

Religious belief requires a litany of assumptions. Religion preaches a certainty that does not exist. Belief is achieved by faith, not by reason. Two questions to ask about religion are, "Does God actually exist outside the human mind or is He just a figment of human imagination?" and, "Can you cite any plausible evidence that God actually exists?"

"...the prevailing view in modern psychology is that religious belief developed not because of those functions [beliefs and rituals that contribute to social identity] but rather as the automatic byproduct of brain systems that evolved for everyday cognition ... belief in the supernatural is a natural consequence of normal cognitive development, and so it should be no surprise that religion is both pervasive and enduring." (Alcock)

"The evidence that lies before us in great abundance points to organized religion as an expression of tribalism. Every religion teaches its adherents that they are a special fellowship and that their creation story, moral precepts and privilege from divine power are superior to those claimed in other religions. The goal of religion is submission to the will and common good of the tribe." (Wilson)

The impulse for religious advocates to inoculate the world with the word of God has produced countless undesirable consequences. Religious zealots have been unspeakably cruel toward indigenous populations. With total disregard for the history, traditions and beliefs of cultures, the Catholic Church, acting under the presumption of moral superiority and an intolerant, unwavering dogmatism, has arrogantly proclaimed that it is the only path to Heaven. It has inspired missionaries, from the time of its formation to the present, to convert as many people as possible to Catholicism. These missionaries labored under the dubious assumption that anyone who isn't a Christian is doomed.

In their messianic zeal to convert everyone on the planet to Catholicism, missionaries wreaked havoc on native populations, robbed them of unique lifeways and gods and replaced them with Western religious ideology. Native North and South Americans and Hawaiians are just a portion of the many cultures in the world that were victims of overzealous evangelists trying to sell the fantasy of a supernatural world and convert everyone to Christianity.

The religious fervor of Protestant missionaries brought God, greed and grief to native Hawaiians. New England Calvinist proselytizers demeaned the Hawaiian culture, caused Hawaiian women to cover their breasts and forbid dancing the hula, which Calvinists considered shameful. In addition, they brought diseases that decimated the native population.

In her book *Unfamiliar Fishes*, Sarah Vowell documents the evangelical zeal of Protestants trying to convert Hawaiians to Christianity. She cites Acts 16:9 — a biblical call to convert everyone to Christianity — as the "meddler's motto." Theologians refer to this bible verse as the "Macedonian call" because a man from Macedonia prayed to Paul to come to Macedonia and help them.

Vowell wrote,

> "...I have met native Hawaiians who still have a bone to pick with the pope, but for a decidedly different reason than the missionaries. In fact, they identify the Catholic Church as the root cause of the coming of the Catholic-hating Protestant missionaries to Hawaii, citing the papal bull *Inter caetera* (Among other works) of 1493, which charges Spain to Christianize the New World, as the founding document that bestowed moral justification on genocide and conquest."

This papal letter justified missionary conquest, conversion, enslavement and cultural destruction in the name of Christianity.

Religion is a powerful and infatuating factor in the lives of humans. It has the unique quality that allows joy and fear to co-exist — joy in believing in salvation and eternal bliss and fear of a punitive god and eternal damnation. Religion manipulates people who feel isolated, lonely, helpless and anxious into a dependent relationship. Some become emotionally and spiritually overwhelmed by confusing and onerous religious doctrines.

"We are not dealing with the kind of religion that persists or the status of its truth claims — which may be irrelevant for many believers—but with the power of religious symbols and institutions to provide structure and order, and to give purpose in an otherwise meaningful and perhaps terrifying universe." (Kurtz)

Religion argues that morality is considerably dependent on a divine presence. Is that true?

"A community needs ethical people, but does the secular world need religious people? Are the saints really good, is religious piety a requisite for communal virtue, do we need God in order to love our fellow man?" (Gilkey)

"For many, morality requires the worship of God or gods, a set of commandments, the promise of eternal bliss, or the fear of everlasting punishment. The concept of guilt is the core doctrine in Christianity followed by forgiveness, another core attribute, which is the primary antidote to assuage Christians that their God is merciful. The secular humanist, whether agnostic or atheist, leaves aside these speculations, pieties, and rituals of the religious and focuses on the readily evident feelings of compassion. Any moral code not grounded in feelings of compassion is suspect." (Agnitti)

Religion prospers because of the anxiety humans have about unknown future events. Some people will always need a god figure to serve as spiritual fulfillment.

"Men need God because their precarious and contingent lives can find final significance only in His almighty and eternal purposes and because their fragmentary selves must find their ultimate center only in His transcendent love." (Gilkey)

The idea of a divine benevolent deity has a calming influence. Religion offers a handy guide for life for those willing to outsource their independence and original thought process.

The pageantry associated with elaborate Catholic rituals and ceremonies lends an aura of realism and authenticity to the doctrines being celebrated. Often these pageantries take place in imposing, majestic churches or cathedrals. The priest is usually attired in ornate decorative vestments representing ancient traditions, standing in front of an altar adorned with glowing candles, gold chalices, bread, wine in crystal cruets and attended by young boy and girl acolytes. Choirs are singing, incense is burning, organs are playing, holy water is sprayed on the congregation and everyone prays for salvation. The laity in the pews are alternately sitting, standing and kneeling between processions to the front of the church for blessings or communion.

If you are raised observing this solemnity and grandeur, the pageantry tends to reinforce belief in basic church doctrines and argues for a divine culture. The evocative imagery suggested by this display of pomp and ceremony, attended by many people, lends an aura of authenticity to religious services.

## Pondering the Inscrutible Mystery of Faith

Most of us will at some time in our lives suffer from illness or infirmities — unpleasant, painful experiences. Yet the Catholic Church teaches that suffering has a redemptive quality and can function as partial atonement for our sins. Pain and misery were seen as punishment for sin during the Dark Ages, and a spiritual experience of purging that smoothed the path to salvation.

The Church considers suffering a consequence of original sin (*Catechism of the Catholic Church*, #1521). According to the Church, our infirmities can be traced to the mythical figure of Eve who committed a mythical sin in a mythical garden. A. M. Roguet, a Dominican priest, writes that, ". . . there is certainly a connection between sin and sickness in general. Both are the work of the devil." Connecting sin and suffering to a myth is a fragile justification for one of the central beliefs of the Catholic Church.

It is fascinating that Christianity grew from humble beginnings to an enormous moral and intellectual ideology, a religious inspiration for life and eventually a symbolic recognition of Western culture.

"The Christian injunction to love and serve all humanity and high valuation of the individual human soul now stood in sharp counterpoint to Christianity's long history of bigotry and violent intolerance — its forcible conversion of other peoples, its ruthless suppression of other cultural perspectives, its persecutions of heretics, its crusades against Moslems, its oppression of Jews, its depreciation of women's spirituality and exclusion of women from positions of religious authority, its association with slavery and colonialist exploitation, its pervasive spirit of prejudice and religious arrogance maintained against all those outside the fold. Measured by its own standards, Christianity fell woefully short of ethical greatness, and many alternative systems, from ancient Stoicism to modern liberalism and socialism, seemed to provide equally inspiring programs for human activity without the baggage of implausible supernatural belief." (Tarnas)

Catholicism teaches that at some point in the future, God will victoriously return to the Earth and, depending on what part of the Bible you read, preside over many years of either chaos or peace. He is scheduled to arrive either with blaring trumpets and choirs of singing angels or in the middle of the night without warning. I believe an appropriate musical theme for the saintly angels would be the lyrics to the Christmas song, *Santa Claus is Coming to Town!*

> He's making a list, he's checking it twice
> He's going to find out who's naughty or nice.
> He knows when you are sleeping,
> He knows when you're awake,
> He knows when you've been bad or good,
> and be good for goodness sake!
> Santa Claus is coming to town!

Replace "Santa Claus" with "Jesus Christ" in the lyrics and retain the same music. I think that about covers the concept of God and his relationship with His creations!

A curious effect that religion has on some devotees is that they believe they have developed a reciprocal, familial relationship with their mysterious God. Their lives are guided by an imaginary deity. Mysterious relationships among humans are common; between humans and deities, less so.

Religion begins where reason ends. There is a puzzling and disturbing pathology in religion in the belief that there is an invisible and unknown force that exists in an unknown place and was responsible for the creation of the Earth and its inhabitants. Pledging allegiance to an invisible leader who has never been seen and who may not exist at all is irrational.

The long arc of religious belief extends from faith at one end to reason at the other. At the faith end of the arc is a commitment to trust and confidence in the unseen and the unknown — a spiritual wager on the existence of a God figure. At the reason end of the arc is unfettered confidence and certain faith in reality, common sense, experience and observation — belief in objective reality. Trust and hope are the requisite ingredients for faith while logic and objectivity are the fundamental anchors for reason.

Faith demands a blind adherence to illogical doctrines, and is concerned with things that are neither real or tangible. It is quite possible that a double martini at the end of the day may be more efficacious than religion to lessen the effect of the tribulations and anxieties of the day, introduce a tranquil nighttime serenity and prepare the mind for the challenges of tomorrow. The effects of the martini are obvious and pleasant; a tangible outcome sadly lacking in religion. ◆

# A CHURCH IN PERIL

# CHAPTER NINE:
# Holy Pedophilia:
# Priests or Perverts?

**The Catholic Church** has become relevant again, but for all the wrong reasons. In the past several decades, the Catholic priesthood has become infested with a dark, nightmarish culture of evil perpetrated by the debauchery of a group of immoral priests committing unspeakable, inhumane sexual abuses against children with the acquiescence of their peers in the fraternity of the anointed priesthood, while their superiors turned a blind eye.

The moral disparity between celibate priests and pervert priests is a chasm of colossal dimensions. It is difficult to imagine men of God and child abusers both wearing Roman collars, inhabiting the same space and conducting the same religious ceremonies under the umbrella of Catholic ministry. Both may claim to be Roman Catholic priests, but they occupy extremely different moral realities.

# A CHURCH IN PERIL

"It is very disorienting when those who are supposed to be our highest moral exemplars have no morals — not even of the alley-cat variety. During the sexual abuse scandal in the Catholic Church, it was stunning to see wide swaths of clergymen, responsible for teaching children right from wrong, perverting right and wrong" (Dowd).

The pedophilia scandal is a profoundly disturbing deterioration in the piety of the priesthood. The priestly caste has become dissociated from those they are supposed to serve. The trust among the faithful that their children would be safe with Catholic clergy has been permanently shattered. Religious morality has now become an oxymoron. The idea that morality required a religious component is shown by the actions of pedophile priests to be erroneous.

We are witnessing a pandemic of abuse in the Catholic priesthood. Calculatingly concealed in clerical garb, a palpable presence of evil insinuated itself into the Catholic ministry. Priests are committing the most heinous crimes against children, all the while preaching the love and goodness of God and the benefits of being a good Catholic.

The Catholic priesthood has been infected with evil men masquerading as holy prelates, all the while molesting innocent children to satisfy their own selfish sexual compulsions; a callous inversion of the pious priesthood. Priests are sabotaging the institutional structure of the Church from within. The reputation of the Catholic Church as a holy institution representing God on Earth has been permanently fractured. The questions are urgent, the stakes are high and solutions are nowhere in sight.

In spite of the Pope's pious incantations, the stark reality is that the Catholic ministry is infested with corrupt men who molest children using their cassocks as camouflage to cover their misdeeds. Pedophilia has nothing to do with God. The deeply disordered men who committed dehumanizing criminal acts against children are not priests, but perverts. Their destructive behavior is a stellar example of a malevolent outcome of the flawed recruiting process for the Catholic seminary.

These priests succumbed to their worst impulses. They would be misfits in any organization but their presence in a religious institution is particularly distressing. The mystique of the Catholic priest as a chaste, spiritual emissary of God has been irrevocably tarnished and their transgressions threaten the survival of the Church. They represent a menace unparalleled in Church history.

The stunning discovery, over the past few decades, that the Catholic priesthood has been  inhabited by a significant number of child molesters who abused thousands of children was a catastrophic revelation that calls into question the moral authority of the Church. The world is witnessing a real-life medieval morality play, pitting good versus evil, in the Roman Catholic Church. The Church is confronting an existential crisis that threatens its very survival as a religious institution.

The discovery that ordained men were ministering to God's faithful even while committing their sexual aberrations was met with moral outrage by congregations and a protective posture by their fellow clergy and the Church hierarchy. That the bishops mounted a stealth campaign to shield the predators and cover up incidents of abuse makes them equally culpable. Their convenient, deliberate blindness to the culture of predation in the Catholic Church makes them correspondingly complicit. The malice of their concealment is inexcusable. Sexual predators in the Church tormented children, damaged parishes and destroyed lives. Their unthinkable perversions led to gross irresponsibility by those in positions of authority. The faithful laity suffer palpable emotional and spiritual overload as accusations continue to be made public.

The traditional Catholic priest has been described by Roguet as ". . . an intermediary between God and men, having the double duty of taking up to God the appeals, prayers, thanksgiving, and praise of men, and of bringing down to mankind the benefits of God." He also writes that priests belong to both human and divine domains and act as a bridge between Earth and Heaven. This previous stereotype of priests as messengers of God has been permanently shattered and points to a deeply flawed body of men. The scandal represents a sea change in the history of the Catholic Church unmatched since the Protestant Reformation. The piety, dignity and integrity of the priesthood are incredibly damaged; and most likely irreparable.

# A CHURCH IN PERIL

James Carroll (author, historian, journalist and Paulist priest from 1969-74), has called for abolishing the priesthood. He believes that Catholics should detach themselves from the "diseased model of the Church" and have the Church administered by lay people. "The Church I foresee will be governed by laypeople although the verb 'govern' may apply less than 'serve.'"

The tawdry abuses in the Church by priests have roiled the faithful. The discovery of a troubled culture within the ranks of the priesthood has a chilling and confusing effect on lifetime Catholics who historically held priests in high esteem as embodiments of Christ himself.

The priest abusers violated a sacred trust and demonstrated a flagrant disrespect for their religious vows and their young victims. Their depravity is inexcusable under any circumstances, but notably moreso when perpetrated under the camouflage of clergy. Because of the scandal, the Church has become an institutionalized piñata, inviting vigorous swings from media, believers, clergy and even non-believers.

The pedophilia crisis is hard to imagine, impossible to ignore and an institutional catastrophe. Church leadership is at a loss on how to rid the Church of sexual predators. Rather than acting swiftly with corrective, fundamental, systemic change, the Vatican has attempted to solve the problem internally. It has become defensive, insular and protective of perpetrators and their enablers, who chose to cover up the events rather than addressing the issue.

There has been complicity among ordained clergy to conceal the magnitude of the problem. There is a depressing irony in the Vatican practicing *omerta*, the Italian mafia code of silence! The Vatican strategy of defensive maneuvering to protect the priestly fraternity is having the effect of airbrushing immorality. Within the priesthood is a perverse homogeneity of thought and action that acts as a protective shield for the perpetrators.

Perhaps we should not have been shocked that priests should react in this way. They have been encased in a fraternal cocoon for their entire adult lives. But the collective arrogance exhibited by the Vatican in its deafeningly silent response to the scandal is unacceptable. Priests were not held accountable for their acts of moral dereliction by their peers or their superiors. Only when civilian prosecutors stepped in were punishments administered.

There is a casual bigotry in the way victims of this scandal have been treated. The Church's reaction to the crisis is driven by its own self-interests and not the interests of victim children or their families. Noticeably absent in rare communications from the Vatican are any signs of compassion or empathy for the victims. The Vatican has failed to express sincere remorse for the actions of the abusers, issuing only perfunctory rhetoric of regret. Victims are denied the simple courtesy of sincere apologies for their painful experiences. The Church has not shown any pretense of moral decency, remuneration or responsibility toward the victim community.

The Vatican leadership appears tone deaf, unmoored from reality and insensitive to the casualties. The response to the scandal was, at best, befuddled and, at worst, wrongheaded. The Church can no longer be trusted as guardians of children. Offending priests showed a callous disregard for the innocence, fragility and aspirations of virginal young lives. The abused children were powerless to resist the advances of older religious authority figures. The rituals, traditions, and institutional processes are all called into question.

What began as disturbing allegations is now a full-fledged abomination — a train wreck with the attendant trauma, chaos and victims. An insidious injustice lurks in the Catholic Church — a corrosive blight that may be fatal. In a Church that requires sexual self-control of the laity, sexual predators operating within the Church hierarchy are being protected. Is this catastrophe a crisis of religious doctrine, a human resources glitch, or the breakdown of the administration of the Catholic Church? Is this a secular issue or a religious issue? The irony is that we are witnessing a salacious sex scandal in an institution distinguished for its policy of clerical celibacy and strict sexual rules for the laity.

Practicing Catholics are still struggling to comprehend the scandal. For pious Catholics, the turmoil in the Church is spiritually disorienting. The moral framework depended on by devout Catholics is permanently shattered. The faithful have become cynical, disenchanted and palpably frustrated with the cavalier approach to dealing with the miscreants. Questioning ecclesiastical leadership morphed into mistrust as the magnitude of the scandal unfolded.

We are witnessing the dissolution of Catholic culture and the destabilization of a storied institution. The laity is morally outraged, the Church fragmented and polarized. The Church is out of touch with reality, and its moral authority called into question. It has been corrupted by immoral churchmen, and the cover up by their superiors in dealing with a criminal predator population exposes the hypocrisy of an institution valuing tribalism, peer loyalty and fraternal bonds over human decency.

We are observing four tragedies: abusive acts of sexual predator priests; the cover-up of these crimes by bishops; bungling, inadequate explanations for the crisis; and the lack of a dynamic solution. In response to criticism that Catholic hierarchy should have acted more quickly and decisively to remove priests accused of sexual misconduct, bishops have responded that the hierarchy was unaware until recent years of the danger of shuffling priests from one parish to another and concealing the priest's problems from those they served.

Cardinal Roger Mahoney of the Archdiocese of Los Angeles, declared: "We have said repeatedly that . . . our understanding of this problem and the way it's dealt with today evolved, and that in those years ago, decades ago, people didn't realize how serious this was, and so, rather than pulling people out of ministry directly and fully, they were moved." (John Jay Report)

Despite this proclamation, sexual molestation of children by adults has always been considered a serious, criminal issue and this lame excuse by the Church only reinforces the notion that the Church adopts a defensive posture in an effort to conceal the truth from parishioners and the general public.

The Catholic Church believes it is "the one true church," founded by Jesus of Nazareth. However, it has a significant design flaw. A troublesome dichotomy separates priests from laity, teaching that priests and their leaders are superior to the membership — a thinly disguised contempt of the laity by the anointed elite. The pedophilia scandal has exposed this vulnerability. This thoughtless, selfish antipathy of priests toward the laity created a culture of neglect in the Church, where protection of the priesthood was paramount to the mission of serving the people. Institutions sometimes forget their basic mission in attempts at self-preservation.

Among elite professionals there can develop an esprit de corps that ignores the constituency it serves in order to protect malefactors within its ranks. In the case of the Church, this organizational disregard of its faith community is called clericalism — a group solidarity in which religious ministers bond in a fraternal relationship. Clericalism in the modern world is ". . . the erroneous belief that clerics form a special elite within the Church and that because of their powers as sacramental ministers, they are superior to the laity, are deserving of special and preferential treatment and finally, have a closer relationship to God." (Podles)

Predatory priests in the Catholic Church committed their acts under a protective, fraternal umbrella of fellow priests. Even when discovered, they were not disciplined. This unquestioning allegiance among the priesthood portrays a poverty of morality within the Church. Because of their unique commitment of mind and body to a common ideology — service to a transcendental God — priests have a sympathetic identification with each other and are intensely protective of that relationship. The exalted vision that ordained ministers of the Church have of themselves precludes swift punishment of offending priests.

The solidarity displayed by bishops in their misguided effort to cover up the misdeeds of their fellow priests was an elaborate, imprudent attempt to deceive congregations and avoid prosecutions of priests in the criminal justice system. Bishops are merely promoted priests, indoctrinated since seminary days to be obedient to Rome. It seems obvious that an invisible Vatican hand instituted a strategic plan to prevent the laity and general public from discovering the breadth and depth of the scandal.

"The abusers were sexually vicious and exploitative but the bishops coolly and deliberately ignored victims and constructed elaborate schemes to keep abusers in the priesthood where they had the opportunity to abuse again. The hard-heartedness and manipulativeness of seemingly rational men in responsible positions are perhaps in an objective view even more disturbing than the lust for sex and control that the abusers displayed." (Podles)

When viewing the Church's response to the pedophilia scandal, one gets the impression of a sense of paralysis in the hierarchy — a failure to fully comprehend the seriousness of the situation and an inability to formulate a solution. The Church fumbled its response to the scandal, failing to address the gravity of the situation. There was a systemic misunderstanding of the magnitude of the scandal and downstream consequences.

The largely defensive response to the scandal is incontrovertible evidence that the self-interests of the priesthood are paramount in the Catholic Church, and the welfare of the victims and faithful in the pews are subordinate. The insulated lives of the priests contributed to the predicament they have caused. The faulty acoustics in the Vatican seem unable to pick up the shrill, penetrating expressions and tones of outrage being expressed by the victims, laity and the public.

Vatican leadership does not comprehend the collateral consequences of inaction. Embracing moral relativism — a philosophy that denies moral absolutes — Church authorities and the abuser priests as well are able to reconcile their deviant activities by resorting to distorted philosophical arguments that allow individuals to express their own version of a morality not subject to critical evaluation by others. But it is difficult to rationalize, at any level of morality, priests doing reprehensible things to innocent children. The response from the Vatican to the scandal makes one wonder if there is sentient life in the Curia.

"The Vatican helped set the stage for the abuse by cultivating a clericalist mentality that saw the clergy as the real Church, and making the purpose of cannon law the protection of the rights and reputation of the clergy, not the protection of children from abuse. The Vatican — and this means Pope Paul VI and Pope John Paul II — sought to maintain a façade of institutional unity

by tolerating heresy, dissent, and immorality, and got a Church (at
least in the United States) in which the laity mistrusted priests,
bishops, and popes; the priests mistrusted the laity and bishops;
the bishops mistrusted the laity, priests, and the Vatican." (Podles)

Outrage is growing among the laity concerning injustices perpetrated by
deviant priests. Their insistent demand for priestly accountability has been
stonewalled by the Vatican, showing a wanton disregard for victims and
their families.

The conventional response to abuses discovered was to reassign the
offender to another parish. Victims were ignored, the "problem" was
transferred to another jurisdiction and hidden from the public and civil
prosecutors — free to continue predation at another location. Victims
were neglected by the Church, but the unifying fraternity among ordained
priests was preserved. This approach demonstrated an arrogance among the
bishops, a lack of compassion and empathy for the victims, sympathy for the
offending pedophiles and disrespect and contempt for Catholic churchgoers.

In an attempt to save the Church from embarrassment, an elaborate
program of deception was launched.

". . . the Catholic Church has suffered from a universal dynamic
in which a group seeks to protect its leaders and views any
criticism of them a disturbances of group harmony and hates any
critics as troublemakers. The Catholic clergy will never have an
open, constructive dialog with the faithful because the anointed
priesthood believes they have been chosen by God and given divine
authority to defend the core beliefs of Catholicism." (Podles)

Bishops and Vatican authorities deceived both themselves and the public. The
magnitude of the scandal staggers the imagination. It is reported that sexual
abuse by priests has occurred in 28 countries. A research study commissioned
by the U.S. Conference of Catholic Bishops and conducted by the John Jay
College of Criminal Justice discovered that between 1950 and 2002 over 10,667
individuals made allegations of child sexual abuse. The dioceses identified 6,700
accusations against 4,392 clergy during the time covered by the study.

# A CHURCH IN PERIL

In August, 2018, the Attorney General of Pennsylvania released a grand jury report that examined 70 years of abuse in six dioceses by more than 300 priests who allegedly molested more than 1,000 victims. Excuses given by the priests for their immoral behavior — quoted in the December 2018 *Harper's Magazine* — shocks the imagination.

"Naïve children need to be educated."

"Touching is a priestly duty."

"Touching is necessary to bless children's organs."

"Touching builds trust."

These flimsy, ludicrous, totally unacceptable responses offer penetrating insight into the mindset of priests who were denied the opportunity to experience sexual reality during their formative years.

The traumatic damage to victims extends beyond those individuals who were violated. Parents, siblings, friends and associates all share the anguish and become victims themselves when a traumatic event occurs to one person.

In a November 20, 2018, *New York Times* editorial, David Brooks reinforced this view::

> "Medication can rebalance chemicals in the brain, but it can't heal the inner self. People who have suffered a trauma — whether it's a sexual assault at work or repeated beatings at home — find that their identity formation has been interrupted and fragmented. Time doesn't flow from one day to the next but circles backward to the bad event. People who endure trauma sometimes say they feel morally tainted."

Respect for religion is deteriorating at a rate never seen in history. There is rage, skepticism and grief among the faithful. Catholics no longer trust the Church. The pedophilia scandal has exposed incompetence and lack of accountability in the Church hierarchy, which seems unable to comprehend the serious nature of an infestation of sexual abusers within the ordained priesthood. Not a week goes by without another incident revealed, and the Vatican continues to offer prayer as the solution.

The cover-up was an effort to protect offenders who were members of the fraternity of priests. And the cover-up is instrumental in undermining the credibility of the Church leadership. Historically, Catholics trusted bishops who govern the Church, but the Church has demonstrated that it is no longer trustworthy. An institution isolated from those it serves and surrounded by mystique invites corruption.

The problem is both a moral and criminal issue. The proper solution is to subject abusive priests to the criminal justice system. It can be sadly noted that exposure of offending priests has been the result of the criminal justice system and not the Church addressing the problem. The complex intractability of the problem calls for a fundamental questioning of the Church's handling of criminal acts committed by ordained clergy. Focusing care and concern outward toward the faithful rather than inward toward offending clergy would be a start. The Vatican appears more interested in protecting priests and bishops than an enlightened push for significant changes in Church procedures.

Andrew Sullivan, a gay Catholic writing in an article in the February 22, 2019, *New York Magazine*, proposed drastic changes to Catholicism to salvage the Church:

"The crisis is so profound, the corruption so deep, the duplicity so brazen that only a radical change will help. Ending mandatory celibacy is no longer an option. It's a necessity. Women need to be brought in to the full sacramental life of the Church. Gay men need to be embraced not as some manifestation of 'intrinsic moral evil' but as human beings made in the image of God and capable of mutual love, care, and support. Gay priests with integrity need to be defended as strongly as the hypocrites need to be exposed and expelled. Francis is nudging the Church toward this more humane and Christian future, but the more he does so, the more fervently this nest of self-haters and bigots will try to destroy him."

A basic principle of management is for organizations to be flexible and capable of adapting to rapidly changing environments. Organizations need to find creative solutions when confronted with turmoil internally or externally.

# A CHURCH IN PERIL

The Catholic Church is obviously not a flexible institution. It is abysmally equipped to deal with a problem as audacious as the pedophilia crisis.

It's morbidly fascinating to watch an institution totally unprepared for scandal of this magnitude. Hallmarks of an effective organization are accountability and transparency. The Catholic Church is deficient in both areas. The Curia is still debating how much truth should be told to the Catholic population. They have insufficient managerial training to cope with untoward events facing them, having always assumed divine assistance would be available.

Many view the current pederasty as something new among the sanctified priesthood, but corrupt priests have been around for a long time. It should come as no surprise that priests violate their vows of chastity and have sex. Scandalous affairs among ministers of the Catholic Church have been going on for centuries and the Vatican hierarchy has turned a blind eye.

"In the eleventh century, St. Peter Damian in his Letter 31, also known as The Book of Gomorrah, wrote to Pope Leo IX of the corruption of the clergy. Peter Damian was concerned with homosexual intercourse among clerics, the abuse of boys, and the degradation of the priesthood. Leo thanked Peter Damian for his efforts but did not follow his advice, setting a bad precedent of papal inaction." (Podles)

Any student of Catholic history can tell you that popes, bishops and priests have been sexually active since the beginning of the Church. The pedophile scandal was hiding in plain sight. A few words whispered at ordination are insufficient to stifle natural human sexual urges. The embarrassing and tragic activities carried on by Vatican prelates, parish priests and bishops over the years has been eloquently and graphically documented in books by Wills and Podles.

On August 4, 2018, *Wall Street Journal* writers Rob Taylor and Francis X. Rocca reported that Pope Francis accepted the resignation of Cardinal Theodore E. McCarrick, Archbishop of Washington, D. C., over allegations of decades of sexual abuse of children. In the September 29/30, 2018, weekend edition, *Wall Street Journal* writers Francis X. Rocca and Ryan Dube reported that Pope Francis defrocked a prominent Chilean priest who was at the center of a sex abuse scandal "for the good of the church." In May the Pope denounced a "culture of abuse in the Chilean church," the latest response to "a global crisis that threatens to engulf his pontificate and distract from his social and economic justice agenda."

The deterioration of trust in the Church has been fomenting for some time, beginning with birth control policies that drove a wedge between celibate priests and sexually active married couples. For many devoted Catholics, disgust over the sex abuse scandal — coupled with growing disillusionment over doctrinal issues — was a tipping point and galvanizing force that caused them to leave the Church.

For pious Catholic, seeking to live their lives in accordance with divine precepts of love and forgiveness with the goal of attaining eternal salvation and moving on to a better place, the scandal has been a sober reminder that human nature is flawed. The sacrament of Holy Orders does not confer perfection on anyone nor does the Roman Collar grant immunity to those that wear it. There has been a steady decline in the confidence of parishioners in the holiness and integrity of the Vatican.

Historically, the Catholic Church has turned a blind eye toward sexual activities among the ordained elite, yet it has dogmatically embraced the idea of ascetic sexual discipline, ignoring the fact that humans are sexual beings and reproduction is the reason that the species is still extant. A church that preaches self-control and sexual repression but is plagued by sexual perverts among its own clergy is a moral absurdity.

Discovering a rational approach to separate carnal sex from spirituality continues to be a complicated issue for Church authorities. "There is a deep and un-Christian cruelty at the heart of the Church's teaching, a bigotry profoundly at odds with the Church's own commitment to seeing every person as worthy of respect, deserving of protection, and made in the image of God." (Sullivan)

The recruitment of adolescents into seminaries to study for the priesthood at the age of 14 or 15 is a significant part of the sexual health problem in the

Church. It is highly unlikely that young men with limited life experiences are adequately prepared to comprehend the consequences of a lifetime as a priest, nor do they have any insight into the rigors of that life. These boys are sexually inexperienced and too young to understand the ramifications of a lifelong commitment to celibacy, isolation from women and living in an all-male environment. They are deprived from expressing their natural sexual instincts and ever having families.

Celibacy is an abnormal condition for humans and places an impossible burden on teenaged boys experiencing puberty. This suppression of the basic, natural male sexual instinct is perverse and may manifest itself in aberrant ways.

According to Carroll, "The repression of desire drove normal erotic urges into a social and psychological netherworld. The celibacy of priests, which grew out of the practice of ascetic monks and hermits, may have been put forward, early on, as a mode of intimacy with God appropriate for a few. But over time the cult of celibacy and virginity developed an inhuman aspect — a broader devaluation and suspicion of bodily experience."

Catholic seminaries impart a cloistered view of reality to young men during their formative years. Isolating seminarians from the realities of living in a diverse society is a disservice to the young men and to the Church they will serve, precluding them from observing the ordinary life of their future constituents. Depriving them of adolescence experiences with women, alcohol, sports and the rigors and love of family life is narrow minded and uncivilized.

Church policy on sexual activities for priests ignores healthy sexuality — the instinctive natural allure of human intimacy. The result is frustrated priests deprived of sexual fulfillment. I believe it is morally offensive to entice young men into seminaries for training for the priesthood before they have fully developed their cognitive skills and matured as sexual beings. The problem now facing the Church grew from the depravation of the natural and intrinsic human requirement for tactile relationships with other human beings.

Although publicity surrounding the pedophile scandal seems overwhelming, there is a lot we don't know about the breadth and depth of the problem. On January 4, 2019, the Associated Press released a story by

Claudia Lauer in which she reported, "Roman Catholic dioceses across the U.S. have released the names of more than 1,000 priests and others accused of sexually abusing children." The story reported that 111 priests were identified in the Jesuit's West Province, which covers nine Western states.

In the April 28, 2019, *Spokesman-Review* (Spokane, Washingon), Shawn Vestal reported that the Oregon Province of the Jesuits settled abuse claims in 2011 for $160 million paid to almost 500 victims. Vestal's scathing report revealed that, beginning in 1970, the Jesuit Oregon Province sent 24 priests accused of abuse to live on the Gonzaga University (GU) campus in Spokane. Homes for retired priests on the GU campus were used to house these priests. Vestal wrote, "The men sent there included several notorious Jesuits with long and publicly documented histories of abuse, many of them in Native communities in Alaska and the West. . . " The President of the University denied he had any knowledge of this.

The article quotes Tim Murphy, an alumnus of GU law school: "The abusers are one problem, but the people acting as a silent ring of protection are just as culpable and should be punished. I have a real problem with the way the Catholic Church has handled this, and Gonzaga's handling mirrors the Church's." Attorneys general have launched statewide investigations in New Jersey, New York, Nebraska, Florida, and Delaware.

Reforms in the U.S. have been put on hold at the request of the Vatican. No reason has been forthcoming. The failure of the Vatican to deal with a substantial gay community within the priesthood — which some call the "Lavender Mafia" — has created an untenable situation.

"We have no reliable figures on just how many priests in the Catholic Church are gay. In the United States, however, where there are 37,000 priests, one independent study has found fewer than 15 percent to be gay, and some have found as many as 60 percent. This fact hangs in the air as a giant, unsustainable paradox. A church that, since 2005 bans priests with 'deep-seated homosexual tendencies' and officially teaches that gay men are 'objectively disordered' and inherently disposed toward 'intrinsic moral evil' is actually composed, in many ways very few other institutions are, of gay men." (Sullivan, *New York Magazine* January 21, 2019)

"After the 'summer of shame,' the case for (the church) being morally compromised hardly needs to be made. About those men trained as priests in the '60s, '70s, and '80s (those darkest of decades), it's tempting to say that the whole generation is compromised. But what if that's true yet also misleads us about the state of the church or the Papacy? The hierarchy could be worse now than it was during the Arian crisis[1], the papacy more compromised than it was at Avignon[2]. I'm just not sure." (Pecknold)

The presence of corruption in the Church is not confined to pedophile priests. The Sistine Chapel Choir, one of the world's oldest choirs, has its own funding scandal. In September, 2018, the *New York Times* reported Vatican prosecutors were looking into possible money laundering, fraud and embezzlement. Choir directors were accused of diverting choir funds to their personal use. In January, 2019, Pope Francis transferred responsibility for the Choir from the Papal household to the Office for the Liturgical Celebrations of the Supreme Pontiff.

It is difficult to keep current on the Church scandals while writing this book. Almost every week there is a fresh allegation of sexual abuse by priests and bishops. On February 5, 2019, the Associated Press reported that Pope Francis acknowledged in a news conference on the papal plane returning to Rome from the United Arab Emirates that priests and bishops were sexually abusing nuns. Some of these abuses can be traced back to the pontificate of Pope Benedict. Cases of sexual abuse of nuns have been reported in India, Africa, Europe and South America.

---

[1] The Arian heresy was a doctrinal dispute over the divinity of Jesus.

[2] Avignon refers to the period from 1309 to 1376 when seven succeeding popes lived in Avignon under the influence of the French crown.

On February 16, 2019, the *New York Times*, under the byline of Elizabeth Dias and Jason Horowitz, reported that Pope Francis "defrocked" Cardinal Theodore E. McCarrick after a Church trial found him guilty of sexually abusing minors and adult seminarians over decades. He was expelled from the Catholic Church. On February 25, 2019, CNN news channel reported that George Pell, former archbishop of Australia and current treasurer of the Vatican, was "found guilty of multiple historical child sex offenses at a secret trial in Melbourne in December." In March, 2019, Pell was sentenced in Australia to six years in jail.

On April 10, 2019, in a stunning, unanticipated and unprecedented departure from Vatican protocol, Emeritus Pope Benedict XVI, one of the Catholic Church's leading theologians, published a 6,000-word letter containing his interpretation and opinion of the clerical abuse perpetrated by priests on minors (catholicnewsagency.com).

Benedict crafted a clever defense of his fellow priests that blames everyone and everything except the Catholic Church and the pedophile priests. He condemns the sexual revolution of the 1960s and a relaxation of Catholic moral theology as the underlying cause of the scandal. According to him, the permissive culture of the '60s and progressive theology of some churchmen led to "relative value judgements."

He writes, ". . . Catholic moral theology suffered a collapse that rendered the Church defenseless against these changes in society." He admits that, ". . . homosexual cliques were established in various seminaries, which acted more or less openly." He cites the Church's perception of criminal law called "guarantorism" that guaranteed the rights of the accused to the extent that "convictions were hardly possible." He denounces the absence of God from society as contributing to the scandal. "Western society is a society in which God is absent in the public sphere and has nothing left to offer it."

This is a seriously flawed letter as well as an unwarranted intrusion on the turf of the current Pope. It is an articulation of the ultra-conservative opinion of a former enforcer of Catholic Church doctrine.

Asked "Why did pedophilia reach such proportions?" he responded, "Ultimately, the reason is the absence of God."

Nowhere does he place any culpability on the priests who committed the crimes. He believes, "The power of evil arises from our refusal to love God."

For Benedict, a world without God has no meaning and no spiritual purpose. ". . . only if there is a Creator God who is good and wants the good — can the life of man also have meaning."

He concludes with his remedy for the problem. "Only obedience and love for our Lord Jesus Christ can point the way. Yes, there is sin in the Church and evil. But even today there is the Holy Church, which is indestructible."

This naïve approach to the scandal only reinforces the notion that the Church is clueless about the problem.

The letter is a classic example of the Church's traditional, unrealistic, spiritual approach to a secular problem. It signals that the Church is lacking the understanding and tools necessary for resolving the dilemma of sexual predators inhabiting the priesthood. Benedict's denunciation of the permissive culture of the '60s in no way excuses crimes against children. He fails to reproach or criticize the predatory priests or superiors who defended them. He shows no remorse for the victims and offers them no empathy or condolences. Rather than responding with a message of sympathy and compassion for the victims, he chooses to use the letter to validate his fraternal relationship with his fellow priests. He even neglects to commend priests who have maintained their vows of celibacy. There is a schizophrenic divide between pedophile priests and those who remain faithful to their vows of chastity.

Nowhere does Benedict shoulder any liability or responsibility for the fiasco even though he was Pope from 2005 to 2013 and before that, a high ranking official in the Vatican Curia. He offers worn-out, insipid, ineffective banalities as a solution. The letter contains no apology, no regrets; only consideration for the offending priests and a defense of the Church. The letter is a self-serving, defensive statement of his conservative views. Once again, we are reminded that the insular nature of the Catholic priesthood is not conducive to the proper management of a large institution.

The saga of the tragedy is hardly over. In the Catholic Church, it is painfully obvious that the Christian message of love and compassion has perished.

The victims of abuse are tragically and irreparably damaged and any realistic remedies and practical solutions seem a long way off. The indecisiveness of the hierarchy will make for prolonged chaos in the Church — institutional trauma that may be terminal. In one of the greatest paradoxes in religious history, the Catholic Church, which for centuries has been ruthless in the pursuit of heretics, is now discovering heretics among the ranks of its own ordained.

Unfortunately, the clergy sexual abuse scandal is not confined to the Catholic Church. On February 10, 2019, the *Houston Chronicle* and *San Antonio Express-News* published an investigative report into widespread sexual abuse within member churches of the Southern Baptist Convention. The report found that since 1998, roughly 380 clergy, lay leaders and volunteers had faced allegations of sexual misconduct, leaving behind over 700 victims. Similar to the Catholic scandal, the Southern Baptist Convention moved sex offenders to other communities and resisted attempts to address the culture of abuse (retrieved from Wikipedia, June 21, 2019).

Thus, we observe and assess the predicament of the Catholic Church: a beleaguered institution suffering an agonizing ideological, liturgical and moral crisis on all levels of the priesthood and assaulted by critics both within and outside. There is an understandably short life expectancy for an institution that is internally eroding and externally criticized. The clergy has been permanently disgraced and dethroned from the pedestal of virtuous emissaries of God. Even those who have maintained their vows have been contaminated by association.

Lame excuses and euphemistic platitudes by the Church hierarchy are nothing more than semantic dances around the facts and cannot conceal the blunt truth that the Catholic Church is infested with priestly perverts. An apocalyptic scenario is playing out in the corridors of the Church. The critical consequences of the shameless deeds of predacious priests radiate out in growing concentric circles, encompassing church authorities, the victims and their families, the laity, the media, law enforcement and the general public. It is hypnotic and fascinating to watch the Church slowly implode because of its own misjudgment, management blunders and internal strife. The long-term damaging effects of these tragedies have only just begun. ❥

# Chapter Ten
# Who Am I to Judge?

**Pope Francis' response** when asked about homosexuals at a press conference in 2013 was, "Who am I to judge?"

This seemingly off-the-cuff remark ignited a theological firestorm among the priesthood and the laity which has not been extinguished, but escalated into a major doctrinal dispute. His statement was a bold, but confusing departure from traditional Catholic teaching. It was a stunning magisterial revision of rigid Church doctrine that historically portrayed homosexuality as an "objective disorder" and homosexual acts as "intrinsically immoral, sinful and contrary to the natural law."

The Pope's remark introduced a new conundrum into Catholic theology: Can the Church allow gay priests to continue to administer the sacraments when traditional Church teaching describes homosexuality as sinful? The Curia, the laity and the general public interpreted this as a significant alteration in the policy of the Catholic Church toward the LGBT community. The Pope, who has become a global media celebrity, purposively or not, provoked a consequential struggle regarding the ideology of the Church.

Francis' agenda for his papacy is difficult to categorize. Those five pithy words, "Who am I to judge?" set the tone for his pontificate. He attaches a "plasticity" to interpretation of traditional Church teachings. His paradoxical taking of liberal and conservative positions coupled with his conflicted positions on homosexuality and marriage are confusing. They present a disquieting ambiguity and metaphysical perplexity between traditional Catholic doctrine and progressive, humanitarian ideals. His puzzling preaching is upsetting liberals and conservatives alike.

At a time in Church history that calls for heroic leadership, we are instead witnessing timid, ambiguous guidance from the Holy See. The Pope seems clueless and ineffective. The front cover of the October 29, 2018, *National Review* portrays a contemplative and preoccupied Francis, chin in hand, in white robe and papal skull cap, with the caption, "The Unheroic Pope." The article by Michael Brendan Dougherty portrays him in an unflattering way, suggesting Francis, "has plunged the Church into acrimony and confusion" with his policies.

The Pope's staffing of the Curia has left many perplexed. Dougherty, in a blistering attack on Francis and the Church, accused the Pope of operating the Vatican with "moral mediocrities, with men who are sexually and financially compromised. There is a type of churchman that Francis seems to favor: the morally compromised and the doctrinally suspect."

As the moral leader of 1.2 billion Catholics in the world, a feckless Francis has reached a watershed moment in his short but turbulent pontificate. What seems to be lacking in the Pope's pronouncements is a sense of authentic moral outrage at the behavior of his priests — there has been no genuine expression of indignation at their libidinous conduct. Examining the ecosystem of the priesthood and removing the tawdry elements would be a good place to start. Without a significant reframing of doctrine and clerical behavior, the Pope may soon be a shepherd without sheep.

"Under Francis the Church now teaches that sometimes God's commandments are simply impossible to follow, that it would be cruel to urge someone to obey them, and that it would be foolish to tell people that God will generously grant them help in actually obeying them." (Dougherty)

Francis appears to want a new, progressive Church — less authoritarian and more humane toward its members. Yet he seems unable, or worse, unwilling, to mount a serious purge of malefactor priests in the Church. His remarks and failure to act decisively suggests a defensive disposition for judging homosexual priests and sex offenders.

Francis' elevation to Pope was originally met with enthusiasm by most Catholics. His symbolic break with past papal tradition was a refreshing approach to start his pontificate. Seemingly indifferent to the traditional trappings of the papacy, he chose to live in a hotel instead of the papal apartment. He eschewed the traditional red shoes worn by those before him. His humility and renunciation of papal trappings made him a global celebrity. The Catholic faithful anticipated a refreshed view of Church doctrines, a cleansing of the priesthood of child abusers, attention to corrupt Vatican financial dealings and a progressive review of dusty Church dogmas.

The enthusiasm for his agenda quickly wore off. His approach to the pedophile scandal has been feeble both in actions and words. He appears defensive and protective of his fellow priests. His ineffective purging of malefactors appears to extend the scandal rather than resolve it.

Pope Francis' instincts are not serving him well. He is administering a consequential papacy, but from all observations he is confused and disorganized. He appears to have underestimated the acrimony his actions would produce. He dropped a metaphysical bombshell on the Vatican and reverberations have not subsided. He apparently miscalculated the furor new policies would generate.

"Ultimately the vision Francis has promoted presents a God who is not merciful but indulgent, even lazy, and indifferent." (Dougherty) Conservatives and liberals alike were galvanized to oppose his pronouncements. He underestimated both the strength of the conservative opposition and the support forthcoming from liberal priests.

We are observing inflexible, pious, religious authorities with conflicting visions of the world, in a contest of perspectives. Francis' autocratic management style has politicized the Church and emboldened opposition from both conservatives and liberals.

Politi, an international expert on the Vatican, writes,

"[Francis'] objective is to involve bishops, clergy, and laity in his project for change. Yet it is difficult to reform the Catholic Church and even more difficult to change its long-standing mechanisms of command. The opponents are tenacious, and behind the scenes their aggressiveness has provoked a growing campaign to make the Pope look illegitimate. Their hope is that the Bergoglio pontificate will end soon."

An October 14, 2018 editorial in the *New York Times* entitled "The Pope Ignores the Damage" reported that the resignation of Cardinal Donald Wuerl, archbishop of Washington, D.C., was accepted by Pope Francis "for the good of the Church." The *Times* editorial pointed out that Francis praised the prelate for his "nobility" in not trying to defend "mistakes" in handling sexual abuse allegations. The editorial reports:

". . . a devastatingly detailed grand jury report on widespread child sex abuse in Pennsylvania churches showed that Cardinal Wuerl, when he was bishop of Pittsburg, was immersed in a clerical culture that hid pedophilic crimes behind euphemisms, conducted unprofessional investigations and evaluations of accused priests, kept acknowledged cases of sex abuse secret from parish communities and avoided reporting the abuse to police. The Pope does not understand the extraordinary damage done by clerics who cruelly and shamelessly abused their power over trusting children and adults."

The editorial concluded the abuse was caused by "a rotten Vatican culture."

In 2018, Francis made public comments on the scandal accusing victims of exaggerating their claims and denying they occurred. He then switched to apologizing for his "tragic error," finally expressing shame and sorrow over the tragedy. Lacking in his public pronouncements was any apology or concern for the victims and their families. Nothing substantial was suggested to prevent further crimes or ridding the priesthood of predators.

The American bishops met in Baltimore in November, 2018, and were expected to vote on a plan to handle the malfeasance in the Church. But they were instructed not to vote on the issue, and informed that the Vatican would handle punishment and accountability issues in Rome at a later date. The Pope is not the cure for the Church, but a symptom of the problem.

"[Pope Francis] will leave behind a Church that is hopelessly politicized, morally lax, and at odds with any traditional Christian understanding of sin and repentance — a Church that has no place for the grace and mercy that lie at the heart of God's demanding love. Francis' "humanitarian" substitute for a recognizably Catholic dispensation will speed up the decline of the Church and the dechristianization of the West." (Mahoney)

"Pope Francis has promoted a doctrinal vision that is "born of the people" in prioritizing the lived experiences and insights of ordinary Catholics over the authoritative teachings of the Church. Calling it "creative fidelity," the pope has defied his predecessors, Pope Emeritus Benedict and Saint Pope John Paul II, who warned of the dangers of embracing the form of "popular Catholicism." (Hendershott)

The Pope's conflicting public pronouncements on humanity are baffling. Writing in the *Wall Street Journal*, on August 3, 2018, Francis X. Rocca quoted Pope Francis' harshly critical view of the death penalty: "(It is) an attack on the inviolability and dignity of the person," and that the Church is working, "with determination for its abolition worldwide." It is incongruous to read about a Pope expressing concern for the dignity of persons on death row while he harbors pedophile priests who have destroyed the dignity and innocence of children.

According to an October 2, 2018, survey conducted by Pew Research Center on Religion and Public Life, American Catholics give Francis negative marks by a two-to-one margin for his handling of the sex abuse scandal. The survey found that, "confidence in the way Pope Francis is handling the crisis has plummeted among U. S. Catholics. . . The declining confidence in Francis' handling of the sex abuse crisis is broad-based, occurring across a wide variety of subgroups of U. S. Catholics."

Media reaction to the problems of the Catholic Church is extensive coverage, with much of it helping to expose wrongdoing and applying pressure to the Church to respond to the scandal. The Vatican's response has been murky, obscure and essentially uninformative.

Francis has only belatedly admitted the seriousness of crimes. His recent pronouncements indicate he may have a growing awareness of the depth of the scandal. In his annual Christmas address to the Vatican Curia, he urged sexual abusers of minors to turn themselves in to civil authorities. "To those who abuse minors I would say this: convert and hand yourself over to human justice and prepare for divine justice."

Continuing to address the issue, he said:

> "The Church will spare no effort to do all that is necessary to bring to justice whosoever has committed such crimes. The Church will never seek to hush up or not take seriously every case. Abusive priests perform abominable acts yet continue to exercise their ministry as if nothing had happened. They have no fear of God or his judgement, but only of being found out and unmasked."

To expect guilty priests to voluntarily turn themselves over for criminal prosecution is preposterous.

In consideration of the pope's words to the Curia, syndicated columnist Diane Dimond in an editorial in the December 30, 2018, *Maui Times*, described his rhetoric, ". . . as a public relation move and a mealy-mouthed response to criminals who have been protected by the Catholic Church for way too long. Does the Pope truly think offending priests are going to suddenly march themselves down to the closest cop shop and confess everything? Get real."

She suggests the Pope order his cardinals, archbishops and bishops to gather up all the known clergy sinners and turn them over to authorities.

Francis admits that because of human shortsightedness, past cases of abuse were treated without the seriousness and promptness due. He affirmed this must never happen again. However, it is doubtful that the Pope has the appetite, resolve or resources to investigate 400,000 priests around the world and identify and purge the abusers — much less the support of his subordinates. The culture of peer loyalty among the ordained will be a major obstacle to any meaningful reform.

The Pope is philosophically hampered from decisive action because of lifelong membership in the fraternity of the priesthood, the intractability of beliefs acquired in a Catholic environment and his experience and associations from years in the Church. A life of prayer is inadequate preparation for leading and managing a 1.2-billion-member organization. Effective leadership requires making courageous decisions that may not be popular. At a time in Church history calling for grit, management acumen, wisdom and grace, Francis has not demonstrated these qualities.

In an editorial in the November 18, 2018 *New York Times*, Ross Douthat described the disagreement within the Church.

> "It is clear that there is a festering sexual and financial corruption in the hierarchy; it is clear that there are problems in the way the Church trains priests and selects bishops. But the Church's theological factions are sufficiently far apart that each would rather do nothing than let the other side lead reform — because the liberals think the conservatives want an inquisition, the conservatives think the liberals want Episcopalianism, and there is some truth in both caricatures."

A December 23, 2018, editorial in the *New York Times* asks if "... Pope Francis and his bishops can investigate themselves and effect the change that is needed." The *Times* editorial suggests that recognition of the problem is insufficient and that the Church, "... need[s] to go beyond contrition and promises, and radically transform the secretive, privileged, all-male clerical culture that controls the Church and that allowed the abuse to proliferate and persist. The Church must confront the clerical culture that spawned the crisis before it destroys the Catholic Church."

In a remarkable eight-page letter dated January 1, 2019, Francis finally scolded U.S. bishops, who were meeting in a spiritual retreat near Chicago. He wrote, "The Church's credibility has been seriously undercut and diminished by these sins and crimes, but even more by the efforts to deny or conceal them." He conceded that, ". . . instead of helping to resolve conflicts . . ," the actions of the Church have ". . . enabled them to fester and cause even greater harm." He admitted that, ". . . restoring credibility will not be accomplished by issuing stern degrees but a solution requires a new approach to management and a change in our mindset."

The Pope acknowledged, "Our Catholicity is at stake." He told the bishops there needs to be change in ". . . our way of praying, our handling of power and money, our exercise of authority and our way of relating to one another and to the world around us." It's time, he said, ". . . to abandon a modus operandi of disparaging, discrediting, playing the victim or the scold in our relationships."

The letter is a welcome and significant turn-around in the Pope's mind-set. He admitted in the letter to "serious mistakes" and asked for forgiveness. Conspicuously absent from his rather blunt letter, however, was any advice on how to accomplish the goals he set forth.

Writing on the Catholic News Agency website on January 4, 2019, Ed Condon addressed the scandal: "It has been obvious to most observers that no new policy, structure or process can answer what is essentially a crisis of sin." He calls the situation a "web of intersecting crises," citing serious problems with clericalism, sexual permissiveness, moral indifference and administrative negligence.

Many ills confronting the Catholic Church are results of its administrative organization. The Catholic Church is is not a democracy, but a top-down aristocracy. It is asymmetrically unbalanced, with power disproportionally distributed to the ordained elite and believers controlled by the policies and edicts of the Church. The Pope, cardinals, bishops and priests who dominate the Church were not voted into their positions, but ordained and appointed by their peers without any input from the laity. Millions of devout Catholics have no voice in the management or direction of the Church, and there is no apparent allegiance to the Church's constituency by the privileged ruling class.

It is supremely ironic that, in the birthplace of opera, we are watching an *opera buffa* (comic opera) performed at the Vatican theater. The Church seemingly lurches from one scandal to another, lacking a moral compass or positive direction. It is led by a pope adrift in ambiguity and neither able to articulate a coherent vision of the Church's mission and future nor restore discipline and moral values within the priestly ranks.

The pedophilia scandal is only one segment of the unfolding crisis Pope Francis inherited. A fractious liberal-conservative doctrinal dispute continues among the clergy as well as the laity. Calls for the Pope to resign and questions of his integrity and handling of the scandal threatens the institution in a way unseen since the Reformation.

The Pope is essentially presiding over a deep state within the Church that renders the institution unmanageable and the papacy impotent. The Church did not recognize the enormous ramifications of the pedophilia scandal, but it makes sense to now assess the depth of the problem and the current and future damage it can and will cause. However, common sense and reason in the Church have withered from disuse. The Church has lost sight of the values of integrity, decency, civility, honesty and morality. It is absolutely essential to fling open the doors and windows of the Vatican and let the fresh air and sunshine of these values disinfect the building and its inhabitants. ❧

# A CHURCH IN PERIL

# CHAPTER ELEVEN
# The Flight to Secularization

**At first glance** it would seem that religion permeates every nook and cranny of our culture. The U.S. Congress begins its deliberations with prayer. Many meetings begin with prayers. We petition God when misfortune strikes. We extend prayers to those who are suffering. There is a church on every corner in most towns in America. Televangelists regularly appear on TV. Megachurches fill their places of worship every weekend with thousands of followers. Yet, the data paint a very different picture. The country is becoming increasingly secular. The influence of religion in the U. S. is rapidly diminishing.

The disinterest in organized religion by young people is also worldwide. Millennials, disillusioned with institutional religion and its inherent hypocrisy, are not attending church. Politi, an Italian journalist specializing in the Vatican, writes that the greatest challenge facing the Italian Catholic Church is the "steep falloff in participation by young people in institutional Catholicism." He notes that the change of attitude among young women will have a negative effect on the number of future Catholics since intergenerational transmission of religion has always been a female prerogative. "We are witnessing a rising tide of exits from traditional Christianity, a heightened freedom of choice within the religion professed, and heightened subjectivity in deciding of values, rules, and even the physiognomy (appearance) of the divinity, to which the characteristics assigned are often quite indeterminate."

The *Economist* magazine surveyed the religious landscape in the U.S., citing data from Pew Research:

> "The oldest generations are the most religious; the youngest are
> the most nonbelieving. So simple cohort replacement is making
> America more irreligious. Moreover, whereas past generations
> became more religious as they aged, this effect seems to have
> paused: millennials became even less observant between surveys
> in 2007 and 2014. Indeed, people of all generations are leaving
> churches. The Catholic church has suffered the most dramatic
> exodus. Fully 13% of America's population is ex-Catholic: some
> join other churches, but just as many become Nones." (Greene)

According to an April 3, 2019, Gallup podcast. one in three Catholics wants to leave the Church. Gallup also reports that 37 percent of Catholics are re-examining their commitment to the Catholic faith, up from only 22 percent in 2002 (March 13, 2019, news.gallup.com/poll). "The Church, while claiming ongoing membership growth, acknowledged a loss of 2,000 parishes in the United States, a situation repeated in Europe and Australia." (Edwards)

McGowan describes the flight from Christianity toward secularization in the U. S.

> "Three million fewer Americans are attending church each
> year, driving the unaffiliated from eight percent to 23 percent in
> a generation. For millennials that number jumps to 35 percent.
> Twice as many millennials are unaffiliated as their parents'

generation, and three times as many as their grandparents' generation. And early reports of Generation Z, those currently in high school and younger, show that traditional religious identity is on the demographic cusp of vanishing as a significant cultural presence."

An April 18, 2019, Gallup poll revealed that: "The percentage of Americans reporting they belong to a religious institution is at an all-time low." The poll shows: "that the amount of people belonging to a church, synagogue or mosque was at a low average of 50 percent in 2018. Since 1999, there has been a 20 percentage point decline in church membership."

Autocratic religious institutions are vulnerable to corruption from within because they fail to seek and react to criticism and feedback from objective outside observers. The seeds of their own demise may come from policies and traditions that emerge internally and grow unchecked and unaudited. The Roman Catholic Church is one of these institutions.

The Church has all the necessary ingredients for a slow erosion of its moral principles and basic mission, resulting in an eventual collapse. Their recruitment policies were unintentionally designed to attract troubled young men who are unsuitable to be ordained to the priesthood. These men have significantly contributed to the Church's disturbing problem with their immoral behavior. The Church has also failed to adjust to modernity or demonstrate it can improve the lives of the faithful.

I am doubtful the Church has the apparatus necessary to solve its multiple bureaucratic problems. Prayer has not been demonstrated to be a successful solution to solving Catholic Church problems. When the problem is secular and occurring on Earth, an appeal to the supernatural is ineffective.

The Vatican does not have a clear vision or understanding of the contemporary world. They are still tenaciously clinging to an archaic message that has little relevance to current events or modern thinking. An education in theology, Biblical studies and church history as well as a reliance on prayer and an invisible divine hand are not the dynamic management tools and skills needed to confront a catastrophic institutional failure.

# A CHURCH IN PERIL

With the current state of knowledge accumulated through scientific discovery and philosophical advancements, it is baffling that there has not been more vigorous questioning of archaic reasoning and outdated beliefs. Science is capable of examining and illuminating reality and offering plausible explanations for fantasies of a primitive people. The Church's intolerance of divergent views and lack of intellectual curiosity prevents modernization. To continue to preach a religious doctrine based on writings of ancient scribes with primitive, unsophisticated views of the world is insulting to the faithful.

It is axiomatic that optics — perceptions of the public — matter in politics. It is also fundamental that these perceptions have consequences in religious institutions. Currently, the optics of the Catholic Church are shocking and repulsive. What began as a pedophilia scandal — priests sexually abusing young children — has now expanded to priests and bishops sexually abusing nuns. To become relevant again and restore dignity to the Church, Catholicism is going to have to undergo a radical reframing and realignment of priorities. Can the Church abandon an antiquated ideology and preach a pragmatic message of love and human dignity? Not until the current problems are addressed.

A precondition for return to relevance will be a genuine and thorough purging of malefactors within the Church. And any refurbishing of Catholic dogma will require a dramatic paradigm shift. The Church is essentially paralyzed by sacrosanct, immutable doctrines and stagnant dogma that has not changed in centuries. Any change in Catholic doctrine will come at the expense of vitiating core beliefs of Catholicism, some established 2,000 years ago. Altering ancient dogma may bring unsought consequences: revising the mission and purpose of the Church. It will have to discard its focus on the spirit world, the supernatural, the intangible and mythical; and concentrate on pragmatic, observable and material phenomena. Change of this magnitude would be analogous to untying the Gordian Knot. The focus will have to shift from the hereafter to the now and concentrate on planet Earth and the problems facing humanity on a daily basis.

There are ample opportunities to engage people in realistic endeavors to solve problems of the underserved, the disenfranchised, the mentally ill, the homeless and the poor. The planet itself needs attention. The only home we know is in danger of becoming uninhabitable if we do not address the ecological issues of climate change, carbon emissions, deforestation and contaminated water. By refocusing on reality and forsaking faith in an unknown, religion has the potential to reinvent itself and become both spiritually meaningful to its adherents and useful to the people it serves. By building homes, clinics and soup kitchens instead of expensive, ornate, unused churches and cathedrals, religion can contribute to the improvement of society rather than be used as an excuse for warfare and the denigration of those in other belief forums.

A strategic vision focused on constructing a just and decent world where equality prevails and everyone can flourish will energize the laity and make the Church relevant again. Clinging to an outmoded and abstract ideology based on a fantasy afterlife does little to improve the lives of the poor or assuage the anxiety of the world's disparate tribes.

Can the Catholic community undertake this ambitious, monumental restructuring and focus on humanitarian needs and work to improve the human condition? Or, is the belief in the supernatural too ingrained in our DNA and the imagined consequences of abandoning God — or the idea of God — too painful to consider? Is it possible to believe in a cosmic, universal force without the trappings, rigid rules and regulations associated with traditional organized religion? Any meaningful reform will be of heroic proportions — it will involve abandoning spiritual theology and replacing it with the pragmatics of everyday life on Earth.

The Church needs to acknowledge the seriousness of its crises, thoughtfully examine its values and teachings, and develop a plausible strategy for the future. But change of this magnitude is filled with both promise and peril. Reframing Catholicism and its focus on salvation and an after-life could entail focusing instead on the value of humankind on Earth instead of a supernatural deity. Is there sufficient intellectual substance in a secular lifestyle to replace theistic belief for those who do want to change?

Anti-establishment rage is inaudible to Church authorities. The Catholic laity is powerless to effect change in an authoritarian church since the ordained hold all the power. The lack of temerity to challenge Church authority is a result of congregations rendered docile by centuries of being told they were subordinate to the ordained elite. Individual Catholics are currently left with only two options; stay and tolerate Church behavior or vote with their feet and leave.

Prognostication is generally a foolhardy venture and particularly dangerous when dealing with religious issues. However, if we apply the model of secularization of Europe to the U.S., it is reasonable to predict that the influence of organized religion will continue to diminish in the short term, and, in the long run, it will disappear altogether. I believe the revelations of sexual abuse by Catholic priests will continue unabated. There are reports of the same problems in Protestant churches as well. In my experiences teaching organizational dynamics, consulting to businesses and government agencies and as a management executive and corporate observer, I have never seen an institution with a problem as serious as the one now facing the Catholic Church.

On December 23, 2018, the *New York Times* cataloged another example of the breadth of the problem. The Illinois attorney general reported finding nearly 700 priests had been accused of abusing children. At least 16 state attorneys general have opened similar investigations.

The expected response to the Catholic Church scandal that confidence in the Church would decline and members would leave is borne out in empirical polling data. A 2019 Gallop Poll (news.gallup.com/poll) found that the scandal has led 37 percent of U.S. Catholics to question whether they would remain in the Church, up from only 22 percent who felt this way in 2002. Also, "…a record-low 31 percent of U.S. Catholics rate the honesty and ethical standards of the clergy as 'very high' or 'high.'"

Laity confidence in the Church dropped from 52 percent in June 2017 to 44 percent in June 2018. Catholic Church attendance continues to decline. The Poll reported, "In 2018, an average of 36 percent of Catholics reported attending church in the past seven days." Also, according to a General Social Survey (GSS) conducted by the National Opinion Research Group

(NORC) in 2018, 23.15 percent of Americans now claim no religion, as many as there are Evangelicals and Catholics.

It takes a long time to change a tradition that has persisted for 20 centuries. The Catholic Church is not going to cease to exist anytime soon. Rather, it will slowly become marginalized as its doctrines become functionally irrelevant and the façade of a pious priesthood continues to disintegrate. The fluid morality used to excuse the activities of misbehaving priests that emerged in the Church will eventually contribute to its collapse.

Revelations of abuse will expand globally to include a majority of parishes; there will be diminished vocations to the priesthood; priests will continue to leave the Church and the laity will continue to walk away. The Vatican will remain confused. It is ill-equipped with contingency plans and lack the crisis management skills and acumen necessary to handle an institutional catastrophe. The spiritual and moral collapse will be difficult to prevent, much less correct. The final demise will be prolonged, unpredictable and chaotic as divergent values and bitter factions among the priesthood and the laity battle for the soul of Catholicism.

Speculating about the future of religion is precarious, but it would be intellectually lazy to assume that religion will remain static and withstand societal influences. But, the institutional organization and liturgical expressions of Catholicism have been assaulted before. Catholicism has successfully prevailed against efforts in the past at innovative attempts to modify Church doctrine.

Martin Luther made the first major attempt to address defective Catholic practices by beginning the Protestant Reformation. Since then, efforts to alter Church policy by Marxism, humanism, scientism and liberation theology have been successfully thwarted by the Church.

I believe this time, however, that dissidents are using a personal method to express dissatisfaction with religion — they are simply leaving the Church. Modern critics of the Church are not trying to change liturgy or doctrine, but forgoing religion altogether. This is a significant turning point in the role of religion in human life. Critics have decided they no longer need religion in their life. Therefore there is no need to stay and try to promote change from within. The dissidents have decided not to quarrel with the ideology. They just think it makes no sense and is not worthy of argument.

The tide of secularism will continue. As human awareness of the world grows and science slowly erodes mythical beliefs, the transcendental element of religion is being displaced. There is a concurrent recognition of the futility of religious belief. Simple cohort dynamics almost assures membership depletion in the U.S. As mentioned earlier, when elderly Catholic faithful die, they will not be replaced by a younger generation. They are not interested in organized religion.

The closing of Catholic schools is an exemplar of the future of the Church. According to the National Catholic Education Association, one half of Catholic schools in the U.S. have closed since 1960. The primary reason is financial — private Catholic schools are expensive and have to be funded by the parishes they serve. There are no federal tax dollars available. Contributing to the financial crisis is the fact that fewer young women are entering life as nuns, so there is no longer a large supply of inexpensive teachers available to staff the schools. Hiring lay teachers is much more expensive. The fact that more Catholics are sending their kids to public schools contributes to the demise of the Catholic education system in the U. S.

The powerful winds of organized religious are diminishing in the U.S., and around the world, freeing us from theistic narratives about who we are, our place in the universe and our journey to Nirvana. Secularism is attracting more and more followers. It is irrational to continue in an organized religion disparaging the life we have on Earth while we wait for an unsubstantiated future life in a galaxy far, far away!

Spirituality has many dimensions and does not have to include a divine component. You can have a spiritual connection with nature and the cosmos without believing in a virgin birth, original sin, salvation or eternal life. Religion is too abstract, too cluttered with elusive sayings, too vague, too unconvincing and too implausible to attract educated followers. ◆

# CHAPTER TWELVE
# Eulogy for a Church

**These are tumultuous** times in the history of the Roman Catholic Church. It is a church in colossal disarray. We are watching a gigantic, rogue wave of evil and moral decay crash on the shores of the Catholic Church and the powerful, ensuing, immoral undertow is sucking the sanctity out of the house of God. We are witnessing a foundational upheaval of trust and belief in Catholic doctrine, honorable conduct and moral leadership. The historical hegemony of the Church is being relinquished by default.

Metaphysically and ideologically, the Church's ethical authority is being questioned. It has become morally and ethically bankrupt. At a critical point in its history, the Church has nothing meaningful to say, retreating to platitudes and the comfort of nostalgia for the past. In a February 2, 2019, *New York Times* editorial on abortion, Ross Douthat referred to the Catholic Church as, "the ransacked, decaying basilica that is American Catholicism."

# A CHURCH IN PERIL

A disconcerting aura of shame has inserted itself into the Church, causing embarrassment, disgrace and potential collapse.

No thought has been given to the uncertain destiny of the Church or the function and responsibilities of the priesthood. It has been obsessed instead with protecting the ordained child molesters. To build any meaningful future will require a blunt assessment of the present, but the future appears to have been abandoned in lieu of safeguarding the past.

If the Roman Catholic Church is to ever have continuing positive influence on society, it will have to quickly develop a profound message that is motivating and consequential for a modern audience. Uninspiring ancient dogma is withering under the light of modern science. I have a mounting sense that the Catholic Church is overwhelmed by the present combination of crises and will be unable to recover from its current dilemma and regain any significant relevance.

Once a storied institution, Catholicism, present at the birth of modern Christianity, has for centuries occupied the pinnacle of the pantheon of Christian religions, claiming a current membership of 1.2 billion. Like the Titanic, it was believed to be unsinkable. Once thought to be timeless and immutable, it has become unmoored from its prodigious stature. It is now sinking in destructive crises of its own making. Cardinals, bishops and priests are being jailed for wanton child abuse. The Church is devastated by internal strife, the faithful are divided and adrift and the Church's influence is declining in the world.

Discord among the clergy and the faithful is reverberating throughout the Vatican and thousands of parishes around the world. Media coverage seems to signal a requiem for the Church. Catholic schools, churches, convents and monasteries are being shuttered across Europe and the U.S. The scandal is more than a crisis for the Church — it is the dispiriting sense that the Church has begun edging toward a terminal point in its existence.

The time has come for the Catholic Church to take stock of its doctrines, its relationship with its constituents, its clergy's marital status, recruitment and training of priests and its relevance in the modern world. It must, with a convincing degree of transparency and credibility, announce where the Church is headed and its plans for regaining the trust of the faithful. The rhetoric emanating from the Vatican is neither clever nor effective. What the Church says matters to the millions of followers all over the world. Its institutional survival is at stake.

Ironically, the future of the Church is predicted in Mark 3:25. This Bible verse accurately describes the current predicament of the Church: "If a house is divided against itself, that house cannot stand."

The Church has enjoyed a dominant influence on world affairs from the early centuries of the current era to the modern age. However, the 17th century Enlightenment began to question both the doctrines and the influence of the Church. The Catholic Church now faces a binary choice: reform to modernity or die. Unless tradition and theology are drastically restructured, the Church is on a road to extinction. Survival will depend on the Church's ability to compete in the modern political and ideological arenas for legitimacy.

Since the beginning of Christianity, mentalities, values and our knowledge of the world have changed drastically. But there is considerable reluctance by the Church to thoughtfully evaluate ancient, outmoded dogmas and learn from previous theological mistakes. The Church was established in antiquity and is evidently stuck there. The Church seems catastrophically out of balance internally and desperately out of touch with the modern world and the needs and desires of the "huddled masses."

Its survival will first depend on its ability to disperse the specter of evil that haunts the institution.

Catholicism has a bizarre biographical narrative. The historical landscape of the Church is littered with human carnage, wrongheaded notions, missteps, arrogance and dubious doctrines. Many sloppy moral equivocations have appeared in Church pronouncements. Like Icarus, the Church has flown too close to the sun of global power and been scorched by its own perplexing political, scientific and doctrinal views. The Church is responsible for unspeakable human misery and suffering, anxiety, guilt and untold deaths. Hanging, burning and drowning witches; relentlessly pursuing and killing heretics; excommunicating apostates; denigrating scientists and scientific discoveries; declaring war on Muslims; proclaiming women as inferior and subject to chronic impurity; condemning homosexuals; enforcing incomprehensible sexual restrictions; disregarding other religions; and arrogantly claiming to be the one true Church.

The irresponsible hubris of the Church has been demonstrated again and again in its views on human sexuality, scientific discoveries, the value and capabilities of women, gender relationships and the functions of nature. In his book *Passions of the Western Mind*, Tarnas eloquently chronicled the multiple failures of the Church to live up to its claim of benevolence and compassion.

"The Vatican curia (bureaucracy) is a dysfunctional caste. The ordained elite in the Vatican curia enjoy a privileged status within the Church formulating and enforcing policy. Since the Catholic Church has a distinct hierarchy with all decisions made by the Pope and his acolytes, the curia is the governing body of the Church. They are isolated in the Vatican, disdainful of the faithful who they are supposed to serve and because of the vows of celibacy, removed from any consequences of the sexual doctrines they formulate."

I believe it would be fitting to redecorate the front doors of the Vatican. They should be remodeled with a prominent welcoming sign reading, "Under New Management." However, at this time, blocs within the Church are competing. Their polarized views are rupturing historical Church dogma. The partisan rancor among the factions almost assures there will not be any consensus on a way forward.

The Pope may be one of the last remaining absolute monarchs. The Catholic Church has a distinct hierarchy with all decision ultimately made by the Pope. Executive and judicial authority are combined in him and his Ex Cathedra (infallible) pronouncements on moral issues. This elitist status creates an unbridgeable chasm between the priesthood and the laity, leading many priests to concentrate on the institutional status of the Church while ignoring the needs and wishes of the faithful. The powerful are leading the powerless.

The turmoil within the Church is causing a cultural schizophrenia. The Vatican response to the current scandals resembles a circular firing squad. Conservative versus liberal arguments are inflammatory and probably irreconcilable. Each side considers the points of the other worthless or pathetic, with perpetual debate favoring neither side. This unproductive dispute is ostensibly between the right and the left but the direction of the discussion is downward. The Church is in urgent need of an emotional, rational and diagnostic renaissance.

The Catholic Church has a dysfunctional fixation on the past — a dogmatic albatross that restricts its flexibility. Remnants of the past — rigid canon established in antiquity — prevent the Church from restating its basic creed.

In a 1948 speech to the House of Commons, Winston Churchill said, "Those who fail to learn from the history are condemned to repeat it." The Catholic Church has not only failed to learn from history but elevated that history to a prominent position and used it to construct the nucleus of Catholic doctrine.

"Religions founded on Bronze Age and medieval understandings of the world are limited in how many belief-upending scientific discoveries they can adjust to before adherents find the constant conflict exhausting." (Edwards) It is difficult to adapt to modernity when captured by a paralyzing nostalgia for the past. Recalling the past is productive if it is analyzed to the benefit of society, but unquestioningly accepting it doesn't work.

The profound question facing the Catholic Church in the modern world is: Can it survive with a fractured and corrupt clergy, ineffective leadership, a disaffected laity, a society losing interest in organized religion and a fragile and outmoded theology? Is the Church capable of meaningful engagement with the modern world and its constituency? Its present position would indicate that is highly unlikely.

# A CHURCH IN PERIL

The Catholic Church elevates the priesthood at the expense of the laity. Using the elaborate theology of the sacrament of Holy Orders, the priests' hands are blessed so they could say Mass and consecrate and distribute the bread and wine used for communion. Only an ordained priest may consecrate bread and wine, converting them into the body and blood of Jesus Christ during Mass. Catholic priests are supposed to be God's representatives on Earth. They hear confessions and have been authorized to absolve sins, administer penance or refuse forgiveness. They establish rules for the laity to live by and counsel them when they have problems or go astray.

Podles calls a lay person converted into a priest an *alter Christus*, another Christ. Holy Orders "imprints an indelible character on the soul enabling the priest to administer the sacraments and confect the Eucharist." He describes this privileged status of the priests as Clericalism. "Clericalism in the modern world is the erroneous belief that clerics form a special elite within the Church and that because of their powers as sacramental ministers, they are superior to the laity, are deserving of special and preferential treatment and, finally, have a closer relationship with God."

It could be argued that the ordained elite have lost focus on the people in the pews they are supposed to support. There is no shared identity between priests and the faithful. As part of the Church hierarchy, priests exert sanctimonious influence while the faithful are marooned at the bottom of the institutional ladder. A more compelling explanation is that attention was never on parishioners in the first place. Instead, the primary motivation for priests has been the preservation of the priesthood fraternity. The priests have their own self-interest and it may or may not include the devoted disciples in the pews.

This bifurcated theological system of elites and lay persons lacks a system of checks and balances. "The clergy should be largely self-governing, but lay involvement is necessary so that clerical self-respect does not turn into clerical arrogance, which inevitably leads to clerical malfeasance." (Podles)

In an address to priests at a Synod in 2018 on *Young People, the Faith and Vocational Discernment*, Pope Francis cited clericalism as one of the problems of Catholicism.

"Clericalism arises from an elitist and exclusivist vision of vocation, that interprets the ministry as a power to be exercised rather than as a free and generous service to be given. This leads us to believe that we belong to a group that has all the answers and no longer needs to listen or learn anything. Clericalism is a perversion and is the root of many evils in the Church."

"Clericalism, with its cult of secrecy, its theological misogyny, its sexual repressiveness, and its hierarchical power based on threats of a doom-laden afterlife, is at the root of Roman Catholic dysfunction. Clericalism is both the underlying cause and the ongoing enabler of the present Catholic catastrophe. Francis has stoutly protected the twin pillars of clericalism — the Church's misogynist exclusion of women from the priesthood and its requirement of celibacy for priests. He has failed to bring lay-people into position of real power. Equality for women as office-holders in the Church has been resisted precisely because it, like an end to priestly celibacy, would bring with it a broad transformation of the entire Catholic ethos... clericalism — the vesting of power in an all-male and celibate clergy is essentially a caste system." (Carroll)

A distinct fault line separates the laity from the ordained elite in the Catholic Church and minimizes any corroboration or productive dialog between the leaders and the led. Both groups are mutually exclusive and currently fragmented. The layers of bureaucracy — with priests, bishops, cardinals stacked above the laity and topped by the Pope — establishes an aristocratic hierarchy that minimizes the voice of the congregations in Church matters. This sort of layering is common in institutions, but the Catholic Church incorporates a spiritual dimension not usually found in secular institutions.

Epochal changes have occurred in society during the past few centuries, reconfiguring societal values, beliefs, ethics, industry and politics. The role of Catholicism, however, has emerged nearly unchanged. Significant cultural adaptation or transformation has been avoided, eschewed in exchange for continued allegiance to archaic doctrines formulated in preliterate times by primitive minds.

The Church has a rigid and distinct hierarchy and a notably conservative culture that discourages individual reflection and reasoning on established doctrine. It has managed to maintain an obsolete theistic world view. It is as if the doctrines of primitive Christianity were cryogenically frozen in an effort to preserve them over time.

"Catholic theology, in freeing itself from its ancient one-sidedness, its long-standing astigmatisms, must suggest ways for men to discern values, distinguish the authentic from the counterfeit, fulfillment from mere aggrandizement, and develop intelligently a sense of direction for working out their destiny in the world." (O'Dea)

In this book, we have reviewed the Church's predicaments concerning doctrine, finances and priestly misbehavior, but a far greater complication is the Church's chronic practice of hypocrisy when dealing with the public, and particularly, the laity. Hypocrisy is one of the least charming attributes of humans, and, when displayed by religious authorities, it is particularly troubling; it is a violation of trust and a distortion of reality.

The Church displays sanctimonious eminence, but beneath that façade is a deceitful motivation to hide facts. The Vatican has been inconsistent in its pronouncements and often employs misdirection and misrepresentation when communicating with Catholics and the general public. Vatican pontification during the pedophile scandal has been unmistakably counterfactual. Catholic Church authorities have betrayed their moral obligation to be truthful. This lack of candor is so prevalent that it has become a predictable component of Church identity. Because of the lack of confidence in Church pronouncements, any perceived effort at reform must be met with a degree of skepticism and scrutiny. This moral ambiguity is a major vulnerability of the Church and will be a significant factor in the collapse of Catholicism.

Institutional corruption within the Church should not come as a surprise to anyone who has studied the history of Catholicism with intellectual curiosity. We are seeing the sordid wreckage of norms; dishonesty, cover-up, deception, criminality and immoral behavior. The Church is burying core values of morality under rocks — and may soon run out of rocks.

Conditions that led to the current crisis have been in place for centuries. The values, norms and behaviors embodied by Church officials have always favored the priestly ordained over the laity and the salvation of the institution over the salvation of the faithful. The distorted incentive to protect the institution and its clerics in spite of heinous criminal acts has led to the dysfunction that we are now witnessing. There is internal conflict and tenuous linkage between the leaders and the led. The Church's historical audacity has devalued its integrity.

We are observing a bitterly divided and poorly led Catholic Church slowly disintegrate. There is a redolence of decadence wafting through Church corridors. Corrupt people in the Church are doing wicked things and there seems to be little interest in a cleansing operation. The Vatican seems intellectually and morally bankrupt. The moral clarity preached by the Church has not been practiced by the Church. There is a serious, strategic failure by Church officials to commit to a safe religious environment for children, plus a complete absence of a moral emotion regarding the victims of pedophilia and their families.

The Church has demonstrated irresponsible stewardship of young Catholics and is no longer competent to have custody of children. The hierarchy of the Church seems pathologically unable to address the criminal issues it faces and is apparently incapable of doing or saying what needs to be said and done.

Two words noticeably absent from the Vatican operations manual are transparency and accountability. The traditional retreat to thoughtful prayer has not worked in the past and is even more unlikely a solution to the present problem. Catholicism is collapsing because of a failure to perform the necessary routine maintenance required by its institutional infrastructure.

# A CHURCH IN PERIL

# CHAPTER THIRTEEN
# Life Beyond Faith

**At some point** in your life you should ask yourself, "What do I want to do with my life and how can I accomplish that goal?" Answering these two questions requires deciding if religion is an important component of your plan. This chapter will attempt to convince readers that abandoning the metaphysical attachment to religious orthodoxy and the associated guilt can lead to a meaningful secular life, conceived, fabricated and practiced by each individual without reliance on the divine.

Catholic guidelines for a living a good life are illogical, unreasonable and arduous. Exact conformance to them involves a stoic acceptance of suffering as a normal function of religious life, rigid rules for deportment and controls over your eating habits and sex life. Suffering is a natural part of living, but it neither atones for sin nor speeds us toward a celestial reward.

The pursuit of happiness is a prominent component in the U.S. Declaration of Independence, but it is conspicuously absent in Catholic doctrine. The Catholic version of happiness is austere and insensible. The Church's harsh tendency for sexual repression, fashioned by two ascetics, teaches that sex is evil and virginity and celibacy are preferred over marriage as lifestyles.

> "When the Catholic imagination, swayed by Augustine, demonized the sexual restlessness built into the human condition, self-denial was put forward as the way to happiness. But sexual renunciation as an ethical standard has collapsed among Catholics, not because of pressures from a hedonistic 'secular' modernity but because of its inhumane and irrational wright." (Carroll)

There is hum-drum monotony in religion for most adults. Repetitious traditional ceremonies and boring, recycled homilies fail to ignite much excitement for those who have seen and heard them for years without visible change or observable results. Required attendance at religious ceremonies is disappointing for believers seeking something. They are finding nothing.

Many of us are born into a collective relationship with a religious community that provides a sense of belonging but tends to limit independent thinking. One puzzle of faith is that unsubstantiated church doctrine is held with considerable conviction by many followers; individuality is regrettably lost.

A remarkable paradox of human culture is the urge to belong to something greater than ourselves, yet still express our individuality and stand apart from the rest of humanity. Religion is a submissive enterprise that diminishes individuality in favor of communal expression. Disciples of Jesus in the Bible were described as sheep following a shepherd, but blind allegiance to a person or idea stifles independence.

We turn to religion believing that therein lies the answer to baffling philosophical questions that have plagued humanity since time began. Pinker, a Harvard cognitive scientist believes:

> "Philosophical problems have a feeling of the divine, and the favorite solution in most times and places is mysticism and religion. The problem with the religious solution was stated by

[American journalist H.L.] Mencken when he wrote, 'Theology is the effort to explain the unknowable in terms of the not worth knowing.' For anyone with a persistent intellectual curiosity, religious explanations are not worth knowing because they pile equally baffling enigmas on top of the original ones."

Many humans are emotional bundles of competing anxieties and aspirations because of religion. They become mesmerized by the superficial promise of a better life but fail to fully understand that promise's fragile support and lack of evidence. The imperative question for those burdened with religious anxiety and uncertainty is: "Should the Church be the custodian of your values?"

The search for joy in life begins with an exit strategy from the attachments to religion. Awaking from a mythical dream and asserting control over your life is a courageous act of freedom and an opportunity to salvage the rest of your days from religious orthodoxy and archaic ideology. Breaking free from servitude to petrified dogma and onerous moral constructs established by the Church can be a liberating experience. However, replacing a long-established philosophy is an enormous undertaking and opening the mind of someone immersed in a religious orthodoxy for a lifetime and exposing them to new avenues of life is an arduous task.

For those wanting a continued fellowship with the Catholic Church, a blunt assessment of the current state of Catholicism may be informative. The Catholic Church has developed into an arrogant, immoral institution with a salvific narrative focused on renunciation of the flesh and tolerance for a temporary life on Earth in hopes of an unknown posthumous life in a place called Heaven. The Church is currently staffed partly by an unknown number of unidentified ministers who are child abusers. Their libidinous activities have been condoned and tolerated by their superiors and they continue to minister at Church ceremonies. It is incomprehensible to me why anyone would want to be associated with an organization with these credentials.

In life we are faced with two sources from which to acquire knowledge — an inner life of the mind and the exterior environment in which we live — an inner self and an outer self. Our inner self is constrained by our individual cognitive capabilities. However, our outer self is only limited by the scope of our curiosity and our willingness to venture forth and intellectually engage with new ideas, experiences, concepts and images of how the world works. These external ventures allow us to reexamine cherished beliefs and compare them with alternative explanations. Investigating ideas antithetical to our traditional views may expand our intellectual universe and reward us with fresh insights on life.

Search for meaning as a necessary ingredient to a happy life is complex and individualistic. Meaning can be pursued on two levels: a semantical approach and an existential approach. A mundane interpretation might be to ask yourself if golf gives meaning to your life? More complicated is the existential question, "Was I created by a God who watches over me?" One uniquely human question each of us has to resolve is, "Does religion and its doctrines play an indispensable role in my life or can I lead a joyful and meaningful life without divine guidance?"

I believe it's absolutely possible to live a meaningful secular life with a compassionate and egalitarian view of humanity without dependence on divinity. To create an authentic, meaningful, productive, enjoyable existence reflective of our individual persona obliges us to commit to an intellectual search of philosophy, religion and science. From these sources, we distill our own version of the meaning of life. This pilgrimage of self-discovery can lead to an innovative world of new ideas resulting in a logical and reasoned concept of authentic identity.

Beliefs accumulated in childhood while listening to authority figures tend to guide our thoughts and actions throughout our lives. But words of authority have no value unless they are supported by facts that are verifiable and repeatable. For many, adolescent religious commitments slowly yield to encroaching doubt and eventual departure from religion. Many of us — but not all — eventually grow out of our cherished childhood illusions.

*Wall Street Journal* columnist Gerald F. Seib reported on June 25, 2019, that Americans are going to church less often — a trend with enormous social and political consequences.

"The steady, long-term decline in church attendance is confirmed in the most recent *Wall Street Journal*/NBC News poll. Just 29 percent of Americans say they attend religious services once a week or more often. That is down from 41 percent in 2000. At the same time the share of Americans saying they never attend religious services has risen to 26 percent, almost double the 14 percent who said so back in 2000. The rise in churchlessness is most dramatic among young Americans. Among those aged 18 to 34, the rate saying they never attend religious services previously was no different from the national rate; now the share of these younger Americans who never attend religious services has more than doubled to 36 percent."

According to an April 25, 2018, Pew Research Center survey, "Seven in ten adults ages 50 and older think all people will ultimately face God's judgement. By contrast, just 56 percent of those in their 30s and 40s and half of adults under 30 (49 percent) say the same."

Religion seems to be baked into human emotion, but what we experience is not necessarily what ought to be or what is beneficial for human contentment. We are unconscious captives of a childhood environment that often continues into adulthood. Young people with little life experience have never empirically observed many of the beliefs they have been taught. They have a juvenile gullibility and are easily convinced of the religious beliefs of their parents, teachers and religious leaders. This makes them particularly vulnerable to the mysteries and magic of religion. Children are exposed to numbing religious platitudes that suppress their natural curiosity.

The powerful circumstances of your birth environment are not immutable and do not need to influence the trajectory of your entire life. Checking the validity of what you have been taught can lead to reevaluation of the elements of your childhood that were major influences in your life and shaped your perspective of the world. Significant meanings that form one stage of your life may not be relevant during another. Reviewing aspects of your early life with a mature attitude and an objective mindset may lead to fresh conclusions;

a psychologically liberating experience. For some, however, a philosophical vision of life and meaning may not be essential and life can be enjoyed simply by experiencing day-to-day living.

Life consists of a series of changes, some positive and beneficial and others negative and detrimental. The pre-Socratic Greek philosopher, Heraclitus of Ephesus (ca. 500 BCE) proclaimed that, "The only constant in life is change."

Many of us seek comfort in habitual, often monotonous routines and resist potential for innovations. However, as we experience the vagaries of life over time, we develop different perspectives and encounter numerous opportunities to substitute new ideas and philosophies for traditional and possibly outmoded perceptions.

These paradigm shifts are challenging but can be rewarding and lead to a happier life. We can resist those opportunities and keep what we believe or make courageous and daring choices that may open new vistas. We can retain our current reasoning or free ourselves from orthodox religious practices.

One way to lead a happy life is to anoint yourself as the authority figure who will be the final arbitrator of what you believe constitutes a happy life. This approach to living does not preclude taking advice from others, but it establishes you as the decision maker as to what makes sense and what is nonsense. Although most of our knowledge comes from second hand sources, it is up to each of us to determine the validity and rationality of the information.

We are the ones who will choose a vision of a world that appeals to us. "The fund of data available to the human mind is of such intricate complexity and diversity that it provides plausible support for many different conceptions of the ultimate nature of reality." (Tarnas) The challenge for us is to employ our imaginations to cobble together an intellectual framework that can assist in choosing among multiple notions of reality. Peanuts character Charlie Brown humorously sums up the problem we face: "In the book of life, the answers are not in the back."

Using common sense, your own experiences and observations and input from others you can fashion a philosophy of life that is meaningful and rewarding. There is no need for divine guidance, reliance on spirits, cosmic personages, mythical deities or religious authorities. You have the capacity to develop an informed ethical framework that can guide your life on your own.

Your control of your life is an exercise in self-expression — the development of your own stable personality based on enlightened thinking and rational decision making. Don't limit your horizons by imitating others or outsourcing your philosophy of living to authority figures. It is your life and you should be the one establishing the guidelines.

Bonnie Ware, a palliative care giver, writes in her book, *The Top 5 Regrets of the Dying*, that the biggest regret of the dying is, "I wish I'd had the courage to live a life true to myself, and not the life others expected of me." That is a sad, poignant and heartbreaking statement of remorse. One motive for examining the secular life is the frustration of having other people telling us how to live our lives. The choices we make have consequences and it may be important to rearrange our values and perceive the world from a different perspective.

Is it possible to feel safe in a chaotic world without relying on divinity? Absolutely. God is a creation of human imagination and there is no need for enlightened humans to continue to rely on a fictional divinity. Understanding yourself is a first step toward emancipation and maturity. It is your life; look around and decide what you want to do with it.

Psychologists and social scientists tell us that we are cognitively lazy. The tendency of our imaginations is to persuade ourselves to believe what we want to be true rather than take the effort of effective reasoning necessary to actually discover the truth. If you need a feasible source to give meaning to your life, I suggest you ignore a hypothetical vision and look to nature for guidance. You are a part of nature and may find meaning in understanding your relationship with the other components in the ecosystem.

In the early 19th century, the philosophical movement Transcendentalism, led by Ralph Waldo Emerson, Henry David Thoreau and other intellectuals, began in New England. "New England transcendentalists stressed individual autonomy and freedom rather than individual isolation or solipsism." (Richardson) Thoreau was enamored all his life with nature as was his mentor and friend Emerson.

"Most interesting of all for Thoreau is Emerson's insistence in Nature on a line of thought as old as classical Stoicism: that the individual, in searching for a reliable ethical standpoint, for an answer to the question of how one should live one's life, had to turn not to God, not to the polis or state, and not to society, but to nature for a suitable answer. Stoicism taught, and Emerson was teaching, that the laws of nature were the same as the laws of human nature and that man could base a good life, a just life, on nature." (Richardson)

The belief in the power of the individual to make decisions was the core belief of Transcendentalism. The movement eventually died out, but the essence of focusing on the individual will always have merit. Eventually the sun will burn out and the universe will end, but those events are way beyond our lifespan of four score and 10, so focus on the now and real and not the later and maybe.

The practical philosophy of Stoicism embraced by Emerson and Thoreau is one of the more suitable options for living a good life without guidance from above. According to Massimo Pigliucci, the theoretical framework for Stoicism "…is the idea that in order to live a good (in the sense of *eudaimonic*[1]) life, one has to understand two things: the nature of the world (and by extension, one's place in it) and the nature of human reasoning (including when it fails, as it so often does)." We come into this world by ourselves and leave by ourselves, but while we are here our success and happiness will be significantly dependent on others. "…we also need some external goods, such as a supportive family and societal environment, some degree of education, health, and wealth, and even some good looks. Crucially then, being able to live a eudaimonic life is not entirely within the grasp of the agent: some luck, in the form of favorable circumstances, is also needed." (Pigliucci)

The simplest approach to enjoying life may be to concentrate on reality. Who and where you are are Buddhist realities. Roman Stoic philosopher

---

[1] *Eudaimonia* is a Greek word translated as "a sense of happiness." The concept was central to the philosophy of Aristotle and the Stoics.

Seneca (4 BCE-65 CE) believed everyone wished to live a happy life but had difficulty perceiving exactly what a happy life is. In his essay, *On the Happy Life* he wrote, "True happiness is to enjoy the present, without anxious dependence on the future." *Carpe diem* is a Latin expression that emphasizes this concept. One should seize the day and not worry about tomorrow. American writer and lecturer Dale Carnegie (1888-1955) defined happiness: "It isn't what you have or who you are or where you are or what you are doing that makes you happy or unhappy. It is what you think about it."

A futile exercise engaged in by humans is trying to find answers to unanswerable questions: the origin of the universe, the existence of God, the essence of the human species, the conflicting concepts of living by faith versus empiric reality. It's a waste of energy to overthink existential questions that have baffled humankind since the beginning of time.

In the 1930s, mathematicians Kurt Gödel and Alan Turing discovered, "... that some statements are impossible to prove true or false — they will always be undecidable." This axiom is appropriate for examining religion. That God exists is essentially unprovable one way or the other and we should not become caught up in trying to understand what is undecidable.

A more rewarding endeavor is to observe our surroundings, assess our beliefs and aspirations and either accept what we have or change it if we are uncomfortable. Life is capricious and wholly indifferent to the human predicament. We live on planet Earth, not somewhere in a distant, unknown galaxy. We live in the here and now, not in the hereafter. An optimistic philosophy of life includes belief in science, the dignity of humanity and the ability of *Homo sapiens* to eventually solve the problems facing the world.

It only makes sense to fashion a philosophy of life using objective rather than imaginary data. What should matter is the everyday experience of living, not the dubious concept that death is the start of an exciting new life. Pondering an uncertain metaphysical future while ignoring the present reality is not a productive use of time.

Many of us had an innate curiosity during childhood about where we came from and how the world works. During the middle segment of our lives, pondering existential mysteries takes a back seat to mowing lawns, shoveling snow, taking kids to soccer games, getting the car repaired and raising a family. In retirement those complicated questions return. There is now time to restart the pondering.

A popular adage claims that wisdom, self-assurance and clarity about life issues come with age. After years of education, observing human nature and experiencing life, one can sometimes gain fresh perspectives into previously held orthodox beliefs with therapeutic self-reflection.

You can't change the circumstances into which you are born, but the childhood environment does not have to control your life forever. Challenging the doctrines of youth is a self-initiated rescue mission freeing you to forge alternative frames of reference. Examining what appear to be sacrosanct doctrinal verities that have been present in a life for years is a place to start.

Many humans suffer from the delusion that the important things in life are just out of reach — or far away — when in fact, they are close by and accessible. Your future is not somewhere out in the cosmos awaiting your arrival. The radius of search for secular meaning in the world need not be vast or reach to the outer edges of the universe. Your immediate environment is an adequate landscape in which to explore for a new lifestyle without a divine element. It's right in front of you waiting to be experienced, explored and enjoyed.

Searching for purpose and meaning in an uncaring world may simply require being content with what we see and have and not cluttering our vision with unattainable material objects or fixation on the supernatural. If you have your health, a good job and a happy family, it doesn't matter much if you don't understand the origin of the universe, where you came from, or the molecular particulars of Darwinian evolution.

In his book, *Enlightenment Now*, Stephan Pinker writes that people everywhere are better off today than they were before the Enlightenment of the 17th century. In an interview with Karen Weintraub in the November 20, 2018, *New York Times*, Pinker explains his optimism: "The most overarching explanation would be that the Enlightenment worked. The idea that if we — being humanity — set ourselves the goal of improving well-being, if we try to figure out how the world works using reason and science, every once in a while, we can succeed."

In September, 2007, Randy Pausch, a professor of computer science at Carnegie Mellon University, gave a famous last lecture to students and faculty after receiving a diagnosis of terminal pancreatic cancer. At the very end of his lecture he explained his view toward living: "It's not about how to achieve your dreams, it's about how to lead your life. If you lead your life the right way, the karma will take care of itself, the dreams will come to you."

"If religiosity will most likely be with us in one form or another in the foreseeable future, can secular and naturalistic substitutes or moral equivalents be developed for the passionate longing for meaning? Can new symbols to inspire meaning and hope be devised?" (Kurtz)

Some of the Eastern religions offer effective moral guidance without dependence on divine intervention. Taoists are concerned with nature and its relationship with humankind. "Man is part of nature and will find wisdom and well-being only in harmony with its mysterious powers." (Burke) Buddhists believe that true spirituality begins with acknowledging that humans are temporary beings. The Confucian view of life is a system of ethics and a sense of fellowship with other human beings. The theme running through these Eastern philosophies of life is that human happiness requires developing a harmony with nature and a viable human connection.

Close observation of the fabric of these Eastern beliefs reveals a pragmatic thread — a common sense, rational approach to life stressing a balanced integration with nature and our fellow humans on the planet. Once the supernatural is removed from the equation of life, individuals are free to develop their own idea of human kinship and arrive at a viable understanding of humanity's association with nature. We must be careful about dominating the environment and overindulging our desire for creature comforts by pillaging nature's assets. We don't want to inadvertently design our own extinction. Humans are the only species that can quicken or postpone the extinction of the planet.

# A CHURCH IN PERIL

Happiness is neither a victory to be celebrated nor a distinct destination. Happiness is a life-long journey seeking contentment and pleasure. We can live happy lives if we engage in self-reflection; seek fulfillment with what we have, not what we don't; make responsible decisions based on reason and common sense; and seek meaning in our family, friends and daily living.

Happiness is not the absence of unfortunate events in life, but rather the ability to manage the hazards and persevere. Happiness can be subtly disguised as contentment. Happiness, well-being and prosperity are not based on obsession with success and accumulation of material goods, but on finding purpose in our lives and following our dreams. Happiness perceived from accumulating things is superficial and fleeting.

In *Walden*, Thoreau established the criteria for leading a happy and meaningful life.

"Walden modernizes and extends the idea of freedom by reviving the classical, Stoic emphasis on autarky or self-rule, by domestication into an American context the Hindu concept of the 'final liberation' of the spirit, and by equating freedom with the wildness he understood to be the source and raw material of all civilization and culture. . . The conclusion of Walden is a call to everyone, whatever their present position, whether living alone or in crowds, in the woods or in the city, to have the courage to live a life according to the dictates of the imagination, to live the life one has dreamed." (Richardson)

I believe Henry David Thoreau put life in the proper perspective with his thoughts on his life at Walden Pond: "I learned this, at least, by my experiment, that if one advances confidently in the direction of his dreams, and endeavors to live the life which he has imagined, he will meet with a success unexpected in common hours."

Hopefully, I have conveyed in this book the message that a meaningful and happy life is dependent on having the courage to take control of your particular situation and fashion a life that is rewarding to you and not have it dictated by others. I am aware that there is redundancy in this chapter, but I wanted to present the reader with as many options for a secular life as possible and discuss the many alternatives available to live a life of happiness without divine guidance. You are in control of how much effort you want to expend in developing a philosophy of life.

Let us all strive to be independent, analytical and use our imagination, intellect and creativity to fashion the life we desire. ❧

# A CHURCH IN PERIL

# Epilog

**It's impossible to** know in advance if this book or my previous books, *All Fish Have Bones* and *A Leaf in a Stream*, will influence anyone or cause them to forsake their religious faith and embrace a secular life. However, my goal with these books has not been to impose my opinions on others but to encourage people to critically evaluate religious convictions and commitments to organized religion. I do not possess any certainty that my views of life and the world should be adopted by everyone. Obviously, there are other approaches to living that have merit.

Hopefully some readers will use the data in these books to analyze what they believe and determine if they are comfortable with their current life philosophy. For considerably too much time, I was a *practicing* Catholic, mindlessly attending Sunday Mass as rote habit (missing Mass was considered a mortal sin). The Sabbath is now a day of rest and recreation. If I can prevent someone the senseless practice of routine church attendance and the attendant guilt of religious practice, I will consider my books successful. If I can encourage people to examine and critically think about organized religion and its place in their lives, I will have accomplished my goal.

For many, religion is a very important spiritual element in their lives and I have no interest in demeaning their beliefs. For some, religion performs an important role by providing spiritual nourishment. However, I believe that life is about the reality of love, fear, anxiety, happiness, suffering and discovering a balance among these competing emotions. Religion offers an antidote to these feelings, a fictional drug, an antidepressant concoction designed to help survive the crushing anxieties of living in our complex, frightening, chaotic world. Like all drugs, there are side effects. It also causes fear, anxiety and confusion. I firmly believe that religion causes more problem than it solves.

My wish is that my books will motivate believers to apply common sense and science to analyze the fantasies and myths that persist in religion. In the modern era there is significant enlightenment and information available that expose those illusions. There is ample evidence that irreligion is rising. If these books inspire anyone to reconsider their religious beliefs and leave their religion, then I have been successful.

I sense a growing fatigue with organized religion. It fails to deliver any tangible evidence in support of dubious promises or doctrines grounded mostly in ancient traditions and imagination. Engaging with the world we know and abandoning the idea that another, supernatural, world exists, brings meaning to this life and minimizes the perpetual anxiety associated with believing in a capricious God.

The Catholic Church has become exasperatingly out of touch with its constituents and the world. The feeble outreach offered by the Church to victims of priestly molestation is a feigned and pathetic gesture. The inattention to catastrophic evil in the ranks of Catholic prelates and an outrageous betrayal of the trust of devout followers has fragmented and collapsed a functioning institution. We are watching moral corruption in a religious institution that has claimed a bastion of morality for centuries. Catholicism is on the way to irrelevance, particularly in the U.S.

For those who wish to remain faithful to the Catholic faith, it is instructive to read the opinion of Robert M. Price, writing in *Free Inquiry* (February/March, Vol. 39 No. 2):

"As long as you continue to identify with the disgustingly corrupt institution of the Catholic Church with its lecherous and hypocritical hierarchy, are you not making excuses for it? By protesting that the Church is yours, not that of these Wicked Tenants, aren't you just making it easier for them to continue doing what they have always done? If you offer that excuse for remaining, I even wonder if you really understand what Catholicism is! It is a top-down operation, not a bottom-up one."

This is passionate and compelling rhetoric from a non-Catholic, and a sobering assessment of the current state of affairs in the Church.

This book was written with the goal of encouraging the reader to partake in an analytical soliloquy and challenge the benefits of current religious beliefs; and, if necessary, to adjust and make the necessary corrections that will lead to a greater confidence and understanding of a well-grounded philosophy of life.

Religion socializes us from birth. You boarded the religious train in childhood because of the beliefs of your parents. It is difficult to disembark once the train starts moving. It doesn't make sense, however, to be controlled and influenced your entire life by the whims of other people's opinions, beliefs, judgements and decisions. It may be time to recalibrate the faith of your youth.

We live in a turbulent world and a continuing self-reflection is essential if we are to live meaningful and happy lives. Our minds are our intellectual homes and need periodic refreshing and decluttering. You cannot escape the confines of your mind, but you can periodically conduct a thoughtful examination of what's in there and tidy up accumulated clutter, discarding obsolete and moldy ideas, beliefs and opinions.

Confronting and evaluating a lifetime of religious belief may require uncomfortable reconsiderations of church dogma learned in childhood. It may be challenging to abandon a lifetime belief in a triune God, Jesus Christ, the Virgin Mary, Satan, the Bible and the Holy Ghost, but intellectual growth can begin by challenging cherished religious beliefs and practices. If religion was important to you and gave you a sense of comfort, but now has diminished in your life, it will be necessary to fill the void with secular content.

Non-religion is not a set of shared beliefs, but a worldview that religion is not a necessary element in a life. Where the Church once gave meaning to believers, it will now be up to the individual to consider alternative philosophies of life and choose one that has a personal meaning for them. New discoveries will open new vistas on life. Meaning in life does not disappear when one exits religion.

There can be unexpected pleasure when an enlightened discovery alters the course of one's life and charts a new trajectory. There can be joy and freedom and a wonderful sense of liberation when you begin to think for yourself and take responsibility for your beliefs without divine influence.

Leaving a religious culture does not oblige you to label yourself an atheist. The history of Atheism and intemperate rhetoric used by some of its proponents have caused the term to develop a connotation that is undeserved and not descriptive. "Atheist", although currently an inflammatory term, simply means a person who doesn't believe in God. The opprobrium heaped on the word "atheist" is overwhelming. It may rank close behind "cancer" as one of the most provocative words in the English language. It has an evil, amoral implication but scarcely warrants this copious baggage. You may describe yourself as a non-believer in many ways, but most people I interviewed shy away from the atheist label. One person told my wife she prefers the term "non-theist."

We make many choices in life, but there are some we don't get to make: When, where and to whom we are born and likely when and how we will die. You can't change the circumstances of your birth, but you can engage your intellect, examine your life and change what doesn't make sense to you. Life is seldom an uninterrupted linear event and there are ample opportunities to change the trajectory to what you would like your life to be.

Some may have difficulty filling the void left by becoming non-religious. There may be a fundamental — hopefully temporary — sense of meaninglessness. I suggest exploring secular humanism as an alternative to religion that incorporates reason, common sense, appreciation of science and respect for individuals. Humanism has no orthodoxy, rigid rules, meaningless ceremonies or church attendance required!

The tragedy occurring in the Roman Catholic Church is a pernicious malady that infiltrated a religious culture and caused immense harm. It is the result of a simmering neglect to take action when problems were originally discovered. The Church exhibits a troubling — and somewhat predictable — insouciant reaction to the pedophilia crisis; a disorder resembling autism — detachment from the *body* of the Church and an inability to read the emotions of loyal and devoted Catholics.

People's lives were depersonalized by abusers. The Church did not move swiftly to identify with the victims, demonstrate a personal connection, apologize, express remorse or empathy. They failed. They had a moral choice to make between protecting criminal activities of the clergy or treating the victims. They chose to abandon the victims.

The elitist culture of the ordained priesthood was exposed as a flaw of the Church — a broken institutional tribal mentality. Innocent lives were destroyed. The Church's inertia and naïve response exhibited a failure of its own divine teaching of the worth of every human being. When bold action was needed it was not demonstrated.

Life inside the insular priestly milieu showed a widespread cultural contempt for both the victims and other Church members and a tolerance for systematic and malevolent abuse by a doctrinaire Church hierarchy.

Cognitive dissonance is the inability for the mind to simultaneously hold two opposing thoughts. One cannot accept as true that priests are pious men of God and, at the same time, priests are criminal child abusers. Only one option can be correct. I believe that those who choose to continue to practice Catholicism must develop a degree of amnesia and dyslexia in order to forget the horrible sins of the Church and develop a rationale that allows them to reconcile the endemic Church corruption with the message of Christ.

For me, this is impossible. ◗

# About the Author

**After graduating from** the College of Forestry at the University of Idaho, Dick Sonnichsen worked in the timber industry for a year before being drafted to serve in the U.S. Army. He served in the Counter Intelligence Corps (CIC) from 1961 to 1963. In 1964, he joined the Federal Bureau of Investigation (FBI) and served for thirty years as a Special Agent investigator, Inspector, and senior executive. He retired as the Deputy Assistant Director in charge of the Office of Planning, Evaluation, and Audits.

In 1994, he received the Alva and Gunnar Myrdal Award for Government Service from the American Evaluation Association "in recognition of his career contributions toward making internal evaluation both valued and useful."

After retiring from the FBI, he worked as a management consultant and taught evaluation and social science research methods as an adjunct faculty member at the University of Southern California, Washington Public Affairs Center. He has written four books, co-edited two others, authored numerous articles on internal evaluation and chapters for eight books. He has been a member of the American Evaluation Association, the International Working Group on Evaluation, served on the editorial boards of three evaluation journals, and has spoken and presented evaluation papers in the United States, Canada, Europe and Asia.

He received his undergraduate degree in Forestry from the University of Idaho and Master's and Doctorate degrees in Public Administration from the University of Southern California.

Dick has three adult children. He and his wife Sally divide their time between North Idaho and Maui. ◆

# Acknowledgements

**Writing is a** solitary venture but publishing a professional, well-designed book takes a collaborative team of editors, artists, readers, proofers and photographers. I have been fortunate to have a talented cadre of specialists that transform my rough draft manuscripts into professionally polished books. Without the assistance of these friends and experts my books would not get published.

My editor, Sandy Compton of Blue Creek Press, is the director and coordinator of this process. His expertise in design, editing and the book publication business is invaluable. My daughter, Jennifer Sonnichsen-Parker designs the covers and my hiking friend, Al Thomas takes the photographs on our hikes that adorn the back covers.

Marjolein Groot Nibbelink of Blue Creek Press is responsible for the proofing and discovering and correcting the errors that I missed. My wife Sally read portions of this book and helped me remember accurate Catholic history. ◗

# A CHURCH IN PERIL

# Bibliography

Agnitti, Allen H. "Voices from the Past: Recalling the 'Good, the Beautiful, and the True.'" In *Free Inquiry*, Vol. 38, No.5, August/September.

Alcock, James E. "The God Engine." In *Skeptical Inquirer*, Vol. 42, No. 5, September/October 2018.

Anderson, Bonnie S. & Judith P. Zinsser. *A History of Their Own*. Vols. 1 and II, New York: Harper & Row, 1988.

Athill, Diana. *Somewhere Towards the End*. New York: W. W. Norton & Company, 2008.

Barnes, Michael Horace. *Stages of Thought: The Co-Evolution of Religious Thought and Science*. Oxford: Oxford University Press, 2000.

Bjornerud, Marcia. "Thinking Like a Mountain." In *Sierra*, January/February, 2019.

*Catechism of the Catholic Church*. New York: Doubleday, 1995.

Boyer, Pascal. *The Naturalness of Religious Ideas: A Cognitive Theory of Religion*. Berkley: University of California Press, 1994.

_____. *Religion Explained: The Evolutionary Origins of Religious Thought.* New York: Basic Books, 2001.

Burke, T. Patrick. *The Major Religions.* Cambridge, Massachusetts, Blackwell Publishers, 1996.

Carroll, James. "To Save the Church, Dismantle the Priesthood." *The Atlantic,* June 2019.

Cubitt, Toby S., David Perez-Garcia and Michael Wolf. "The Un(solv)able Problem." *Scientific American,* October, 2018, Vol.319, No. 4.

Davis, Joseph E. "No Country for Old Age." In *the Hedgehog Review.* Fall 2018.

DeConnick, April D. *Holy Misogyny.* New York: The Continuum International Publishing Group, 2011.

Dougherty, Michael Brendan. "The Case Against Pope Francis." In the *National Review,* October 29, 2018.

Dowd, Maureen. "A Down and Dirty White House." *The New York Times,* June 16, 2019.

Edwards, Fred. "Faith and Faithlessness by Generation." In *The Humanist,* Sep./Oct. 2018.

Farris Naff, Clay and Andy Norman. "Getting Real About Right and Wrong." In *Skeptic,* Vol. 23 No. 3, 20118.

Ferguson, Duncan S. *Biblical Hermeneutics.* Eugene, Oregon, WIPF & STOCK, 1986.

Gilkey, Langdon. *Shantung Compound.* New York: Harper One, 1966.

Gray, Stephen B. "Humbling Humanity." In *Skeptic,* Vol 23, No. 2, 2018.

Greene, Lane. "Losing Faith." In *The Economist,* The World in 2019, Fall 2018.

Harari, Yuval Noah. *Homo Deus: A Brief History of Tomorrow.* New York: Harper Collins, 2017.

_____. *21 Lessons for the 21ˢᵗ Century,* New York: Spiegel & Grau, 2018.

Harris, Sam. *The End of Faith: Religion, Terror, and the Future of Reason.* New York: W. W. Norton & Company, 2004.

Hendershott, Anne. "The Crisis of the Catholic Church under Pope Francis." *National Review Symposium,* October 21, 2018. nationalreview.com

John Jay Report. *The Nature and Scope of the Problem of Sexual Abuse of Minors by Catholic Priests and Deacons in the United States.* Posted on the Internet, February 27, 2004.

Kahler, Martin. *So-Called Historical Jesus and the Historical Biblical Christ.* Minneapolis, MN, Fortress Press, 1988.

Kalanithi, Paul. *When Breath Becomes Air.* New York: Random House, 2016.

Kochanski, Daniel. "Why the Catholic Church is so Conflicted about Sex?" In *Humanist Magazine*, January/February 2019.

Kurtz, Paul. "Are Science and Religion Compatible?" In *Skeptical Inquirer*, Vol. 26.2, March/ April, 2000.

_____. "Why Do People Believe or Disbelieve?" In *Science and Religion*, Paul Kurtz (Ed.), Amherst, New York: Prometheus Books, 2003.

Lewis, Ralph. "Persistent of Belief in a Purposeful Universe." In *Skeptic*, Vol. 23, No. 2, 2018.

Mack, Burton L. *The Rise and Fall of the Christian Myth.* New Haven, CT: Yale University Press, 2017.

Mahoney, Daniel J. "The Crisis of the Catholic Church under Pope Francis." *National Review Symposium*, October 21, 2018. nationalreview.com

McClay, Wilfred M. "The Strange Persistence of Guilt." In *The Hedgehog Review*, Spring, 2017.

McGowan, Dale. "As the Christian Church Crumbles, is Humanism Ready to Step Up?" In *the Humanist*, Sep/Oct 2018.

Miles, Jack. *God: A Biography.* New York: Vintage Books, 1996.

Mithen, Steven. *The Prehistory of the Mind.* London: Thames and Hudson, 1996.

O'Dea, Thomas F. *The Catholic Crisis.* Boston: Beacon Press, 1968.

Pecknold, C. C. "The Crisis of the Catholic Church under Pope Francis." *National Review Symposium*, October 21, 2018. nationalreview.com

Pigliucci, Massimo. *How to be a Stoic.* New York: Basic Books 2017.

Pinker, Steven. *How the Mind Works.* New York: W. W. Norton & Company, 1997.

_____. *Enlightenment Now.* New York: Viking Penguin Random House, 2018.

Podles, Leon J. *Sacrilege: Sexual Abuse in the Catholic Church*. Baltimore: Crossland Press, 2008.

Politi, Marco. *Pope Francis Among the Wolves*. New York: Columbia University Press, 2014.

Richardson, Robert D. Jr. *Thoreau: A Life of the Mind*. Berkeley: University of California Press, 1986.

Robinson, Kim Stanley. "There is No Planet B." In *Sierra*, January/February, 2019.

Roguet, A.M. "The Sacraments: The Christian's Journey through Life." In *the Idea of Catholicism*, Walter J. Burghardt, S. J. and William F. Lynch, S.J., Eds. New York, 1960.

Scialabba, George. "Bad Faith." In *The New Republic*. October 1, 2018.

Shermer, Michael. *How We Believe*. New York: W. H. Freeman/Owl Book, 2000.

Sullivan, Andrew. "The Gay Church: Thousands of priests are closeted and the Vatican's failure to reckon with their sexuality has created a crisis for Catholicism." *New York Magazine*, January 21, 2019.

Tarnas, Richard. *The Passion of the Western Mind*. New York: Ballantine Books, 1991.

Vowell, Sarah. *Unfamiliar Fishes*. New York: Riverhead Books, 2011.

Ware, Bonnie. *The Top 5 Regrets of the Dying*. Carlsbad, CA: Hay House, 2012.

Wilber, Ken. *The Marriage of Sense and Soul*. New York: Broadway Books, 1998.

Wills, Garry. *Papal Sin*. New York, Doubleday, 2000.

Wilson, Edward O. *The Social Conquest of Earth*. New York: Liveright Publishing Corporation, 2012.

Made in the USA
Monee, IL
08 September 2020

41304515R00089